Psychology of Human Behavior
Part I

Professor David W. Martin

THE TEACHING COMPANY ®

PUBLISHED BY:

THE TEACHING COMPANY
4151 Lafayette Center Drive, Suite 100
Chantilly, Virginia 20151-1232
1-800-TEACH-12
Fax—703-378-3819
www.teach12.com

ISBN 1-59803-182-1

David W. Martin, Ph.D.
Professor of Psychology, North Carolina State University

David Martin received a B.A. in psychology from Hanover College in Indiana, where he also finished the necessary coursework for a major in physics. He received an M.A. in experimental psychology and a Ph.D. in engineering psychology from The Ohio State University.

Professor Martin began his professional career in 1969 as an assistant professor at New Mexico State University. He progressed through the ranks, becoming a professor in 1983. During this time, Professor Martin contributed to developing a prominent Ph.D. program in engineering psychology. During his final 11 years at NMSU, he was also head of the department. At NMSU, Professor Martin taught courses in introductory psychology, perception, research methods, and human performance; was selected as an outstanding professor by graduating seniors; was named a master teacher; and received a Roush Award for Teaching Excellence. In 1992, Professor Martin assumed his current position as professor and head of the Psychology Department at North Carolina State University. In addition to his administrative duties, he regularly teaches a psychology survey course, an honors seminar, and an evolutionary psychology seminar. He was named to the Academy of Outstanding Teachers at NC State in 1997.

Professor Martin's areas of research in engineering psychology and ergonomics include attention in visual search, particularly in human-computer interaction; operator workload; and cognitive modeling, particularly of human decision making. He has written more than 75 publications and papers. He is the author of *Doing Psychology Experiments*, an experimental methods text currently adopted by more than 100 colleges and in its sixth edition. Dr. Martin has also engaged in considerable professional consulting.

Professor Martin is a member and fellow of the American Psychological Association and a member of the American Psychological Society, the Psychonomic Society, and the Human Factors and Ergonomics Society (HFES). He is a past president of the Rocky Mountain Psychological Association and past president of both the Rio Grande Chapter and the Carolina Chapter of HFES. He has also served for many years on the national committee that designates doctoral psychology programs.

Professor Martin lives in Cary, North Carolina, with his two teenage sons.

Table of Contents

Psychology of Human Behavior
Part I

Psychology of Human Behavior

Scope:

This course of 36 lectures examines the breadth of modern psychology from both clinical and experimental perspectives. After an introduction to the precursors and early history of psychology in Lecture One, we discuss the research methods used in scientific psychology in Lectures Two and Three. Particular emphasis is given to the logic and procedures of the quantitative methods of experimentation, as well as correlational and quasi-experimental design. Consideration is also given to the qualitative designs of ethnography, naturalistic observation, and case history. Following a brief introduction to the scientific theory of evolution in Lecture Four, we discuss a less scientific theory in Lecture Five, that is, psychoanalytic theory as introduced by Sigmund Freud.

In Lectures Seven through Eleven, the topic of abnormal psychology is introduced, and we make a comprehensive examination of the various classifications of mental illness with reference to the *Diagnostic and Statistical Manual of Mental Disorders* (DSM-IV-TR™). For each disorder, we look at the set of defining symptoms and, where known, the causes and prognosis of the illness. In Lectures Twelve through Seventeen, we explore three therapy classifications. For physical therapies, we discuss the various psychopharmacological approaches for each of the disorders, including discussion of electroconvulsive shock therapy and psychosurgeries. Psychotherapies are also covered, with an emphasis on psychoanalysis and humanistic and cognitive therapies. Behavior therapies are also examined, both those based on classical conditioning and those based on operant conditioning.

In Lectures Eighteen through Thirty-One, we examine the standard content areas of experimental scientific psychology. The lecture on motivation emphasizes the biologically based homeostatic model, in which the goal of behavior is the return to an optimal state, although a brief discussion of Abraham Maslow's self-actualization model is also included. The first lecture on motivation emphasizes the difficulty in measuring a private event, such as emotion, and examines the largely unsuccessful attempts of using facial expressions, self-report, and physiological measures, such as the polygraph, pupil size, and vocal tremors. In Lecture Twenty, we consider several theories of emotion, including the James-Lange theory, the Cannon-Bard theory, and Stanley Schachter's cognitive-labeling theory. Lectures Twenty-One and Twenty-Two provide an overview of various psychoactive drugs, including their classifications and behavioral effects.

In Lectures Twenty-Three and Twenty-Four, we introduce the broad area of social psychology, then cover in detail the mechanisms that influence us to behave in automatic ways, as put forth by Robert Cialdini in his book *Influence*. In the next three lectures, Twenty-Five through Twenty-Seven, we examine two forms of simple learning. Classical conditioning involves the pairing of an unconditioned stimulus with a conditioned stimulus, which eventually causes the conditioned stimulus to bring about a conditioned response. Operant conditioning involves repeatedly reinforcing a voluntary response, which increases the probability of the response recurring. For both forms of learning, we detail the time course of learning and the conditions under which learning takes place. In the final learning lecture, we look at progressively more complex forms of learning, such as avoidance learning, probability learning, and concept formation, and consider whether these could be explained as combinations of classical and operant conditioning.

In Lectures Twenty-Eight and Twenty-Nine, we look at memory. First, we consider how the various ways of assessing memory influence how good our memories seem to be. Then, we use an exercise in illusory memory to demonstrate how the modern view of memory is that of constructing memories from cues rather than calling up detailed snapshots. Finally, we review some research that demonstrates how this constructive process can lead to false memories. In the second memory lecture, we learn about some memory aids that can help us improve our memories, and we discuss three theories of forgetting: decay, interference, and consolidation. Perception is covered in Lectures Thirty and Thirty-One. In the first lecture, we use a series of visual illusions to convince ourselves that we are not in direct contact with the external world but that we use cues to form one or more external models that are sometimes in error. In the second lecture, we discuss three schools of thought about how we use cues to form internal models, and we then use the process of depth perception to illustrate what kinds of cues we employ. Finally, we look at evidence supporting the proposition that perception is built in or learned.

Lectures Thirty-Two through Thirty-Four examine modern thought regarding evolutionary psychology. In Lecture Thirty-Two, we discuss the requirements for evolution to take place and some of the myths about evolution. Then, we give a rough timeline of human evolution and look at evolved behavior from the perspective of Desmond Morris's historical book *The Naked Ape*, particularly with respect to why we are naked, why we are sexy, and why human aggression is such a problem. The second evolution lecture examines the topics of altruism and mating. Altruistic behavior includes our behavior toward our kin and reciprocal behavior toward non-kin. Our discussion of mating includes the different behavioral strategies used by men and women related to differences in parental investment in their offspring. In the third evolutionary lecture, aggression is considered, along with parenting and eating behaviors. Evolutionary theory makes specific predictions about the kinds of family conflicts found even in today's families. The reasons we overeat to the point of obesity are also understandable from evolution.

In Lecture Thirty-Five, we look at the applied field of engineering psychology and consider how this field, which is concerned with the design of human-machine-environment, is integrated with other disciplines, such as industrial engineering. We also examine the types of recommendations engineering psychologists can make in the design of displays and controls. In the final lecture, we review where we have been, then briefly discuss a few topics not previously covered, including neuropsychology, cognitive modeling, and developmental psychology. Finally, we consider the future of psychology, with particular emphasis on genetic therapies for mental illnesses and the application of scientific psychology to practical societal problems.

Lecture One
Modern Psychology in Historical Context

Scope:

This lecture introduces psychology as the study of human behavior, either from a clinical or a scientific perspective. It makes the distinction between clinical psychologists (who try to help people with behavioral problems in many settings, such as hospitals, clinics, schools, and prisons) and psychiatrists (who are medical doctors, can prescribe drugs, and are usually trained in a single type of therapy). Clinical psychologists have doctoral degrees, cannot prescribe drugs, and are often trained in a variety of therapies. The lecture also emphasizes the fact that experimental psychologists study human behavior as scientists. We put psychology in a historical perspective by introducing figures who served as precursors in psychology, including philosophers, such as Descartes, Locke, and Hume, and biologists, such as Weber and Darwin. The history of psychology covers only a little more than 100 years and has gone through several methodological approaches. In experimental psychology, the early introspectionists gave way to the behaviorists, who then were largely supplanted by cognitive psychologists. Recently, evolutionary psychologists have offered a new approach. This lecture also previews the topics that are covered in the course and explains why they are ordered as they are.

Outline

I. Psychologists are interested in human behavior, either studying behavior from a scientific perspective or using knowledge gained from the scientific perspective to try to improve the human condition.

    A. About two-thirds of psychologists fit the general label of *clinical psychologist* and are typically interested in helping people with behavioral problems.

        1. Most people think of clinical psychologists as working in private practice one-on-one with clients.

2. Some clinical psychologists work in hospitals, clinics, schools, prisons, and other settings, not only doing therapy but giving tests, evaluating clients, setting up programs, and engaging in other activities to help people.

B. Many people confuse psychiatrists and clinical psychologists.

1. Psychiatrists are medical doctors who can prescribe drugs and give physical exams.

2. Most psychiatrists are trained from a narrow therapeutic orientation, usually psychoanalysis.

3. A clinical psychologist typically has a doctoral degree, usually a Ph.D.

4. Most clinical psychologists cannot prescribe drugs.

5. Clinical psychologists are usually trained to use a wider variety of therapeutic techniques.

C. About one-third of psychologists fit the general label of *experimental psychologist* and are typically interested in studying human behavior from a scientific perspective.

1. Many experimental psychologists work in universities and colleges, both teaching and doing research.

2. Experimental psychologists also work in research institutes for the government, performing both basic and applied research.

3. Increasingly, experimental psychologists work in industry as industrial/organizational psychologists or ergonomists.

II. An understanding of modern psychology requires some knowledge of the history of psychology and major movements in the field.

A. Psychology originally grew out of philosophy and, to some extent, biology; indeed, some philosophical and biological thought still influences psychology.

1. In 1649, René Descartes speculated about the nature of the mind as distinct from the body, with the mind and the idea of self being innate.

2. In 1690, John Locke asserted that the mind is a *tabula rasa*, or blank slate, and all knowledge is gained through experience using the senses.

3. David Hume, working about 1740, was a British associationist who claimed that the mind was no more than a collection of sensory impressions linked together by associations formed by contiguity and similarity.

4. In the 1830s, Ernst Heinrich Weber was one of the first empiricists, who demonstrated the quantification of mental or psychological operations.

5. Charles Darwin in the 1870s applied his theory of evolution to humans.

B. Psychology as a separate discipline began in the latter half of the 1800s.

1. In 1879, Wilhelm Wundt established the first psychological laboratory in Leipzig, Germany.

2. In 1890, William James, although not an empiricist himself, introduced the empirical science of psychology to America.

3. About 1900, Sigmund Freud introduced psychoanalytic theory, giving particular emphasis to the unconscious mind.

4. About 1906, Ivan Pavlov, a physiologist, discovered classical conditioning while studying saliva in dogs.

5. About 1913, John Watson began the behaviorist tradition of psychology, in which behaviors, rather than the conscious mind, are studied.

6. In the 1950s, B. F. Skinner rejected theories of mental operations and argued that only observable behaviors were worth studying.

7. In the 1960s, Ulric Neisser reintroduced the possibility of studying mental operations of the cognitively functioning brain. This approach is called *cognitive psychology* and is still the primary paradigm of psychology today.

8. In 1975, Edward O. Wilson published a book on sociobiology, claiming that evolutionary theory could explain much of human behavior, as well as that of other animals. The evolutionary approach has had some impact since the 1990s.

III. Since its inception as a separate disciplinary field, psychology has undergone some significant changes in theoretical approaches, both in terms of experimental psychology and clinical psychology.

A. Experimental psychology has seen several approaches during a little more than a century.

1. One of the earliest methods used was introspection, in which trained observers attempted to determine the contents of their own minds.

2. The behaviorists claimed that people could not determine the contents of their own minds and that it was impossible to study the workings of the human mind; only observable behaviors could be studied. Because human behavior can be affected by conscious thinking, behaviorist research focused primarily on animal behavior. Behaviorists held sway for 40–60 years, until the arrival of cognitive psychology in the 1960s.

3. The development of the computer influenced the growth of cognitive psychology: Cognitive psychologists believed that it was possible to study the operations of the human mind by using sophisticated research techniques often based on a computer metaphor.

4. Although cognitive psychologists still consider the mind, to some extent, to be a blank slate, evolutionary psychologists claim that the human mind is not a "blank-slate" computer but contains many modules that have been built in to help solve evolutionary problems.

B. Clinical psychology has also seen several trends in its century of existence.

1. Freud proposed that human motivations lie largely at the unconscious level; for this reason, highly trained psychoanalysts must spend many years trying to determine the contents of the unconscious mind in order to help patients.
2. Carl Rogers and other humanistic psychologists proposed that clients have within themselves the ability to analyze and fix their own problems if given proper guidance by a therapist.
3. Behavior therapists believe that many psychological problems are caused by people having learned inappropriate responses to stimuli and that these problems can be solved by having clients learn appropriate responses.
4. Cognitive therapists believe that many psychological problems are caused by people having inappropriate thoughts and that these problems can be corrected by teaching clients to change their thinking.

IV. Psychology today has many sub-areas, most of which we will explore in this course.

A. First, in Lectures Two and Three, we will establish a foundation by looking at some of the research methods used by psychologists.

B. In Lecture Four, we will look at some of the basics of evolutionary theory, because evolutionary theory helps us understand some of the reasons why we behave as we do. I would like you to keep this theory in mind as we explore some of the basic areas of psychology.

C. In Lectures Five and Six, we will examine one of the oldest and most prominent theories of personality, Freud's psychoanalytic theory. I think it is important to understand psychoanalytic theory before covering the various mental illnesses, because to some extent, the classifications of mental illness are loosely based on this theory.

D. In Lectures Seven through Eleven, we will ask why we consider some behaviors to be abnormal and will classify these behaviors into categories of mental illnesses. I have found that it is better to examine abnormal behavior and therapies early in the course because, much as we might learn how a car works when it breaks down, we can learn a good deal about normal behavior by examining abnormal behavior.

E. In Lectures Twelve through Seventeen, we consider three categories of therapies that can be used in treating mental illnesses. I cover these categories separately from the illnesses themselves because, unlike physical illnesses, for which a particular therapy is used to treat a single illness, for mental illnesses, a particular illness might be treated by several different therapies, and the type of therapy chosen is sometimes determined more by the orientation of the therapist than by the illness.

F. In Lectures Eighteen through Twenty-Two, we examine some theories of motivation, that is, what drives us; of emotion, how we feel about events; and of psychoactive drugs, because drugs are a major way of altering our emotions.

G. In Lectures Twenty-Three and Twenty-Four, we look in detail at influence, one of the sub-areas of the very large field of social psychology.

H. In Lectures Twenty-Five through Thirty-One, we explore three of the major research areas of experimental psychology (learning, memory, and perception), emphasizing how our views of these areas have changed in recent years.

I. In Lectures Thirty-Three through Thirty-Four, we use the recently prominent field of evolutionary psychology to help us try to answer questions about why we behave the way we do.

J. In Lecture Thirty-Five, we consider engineering psychology, one of the several fields of applied psychology.

K. In Lecture Thirty-Six, I give a quick review of what we have covered in the course and a thumbnail sketch of several of areas we will not have time to cover in detail, such as neuropsychology, which we will discuss only briefly when we look at psychoactive drugs and drug therapies; cognitive modeling, which we will touch on in the context of complex learning; and developmental psychology, including child psychology and gerontology.

Essential Reading:

D. P. Schultz and S. E. Schultz, *A History of Modern Psychology*, 7th ed.

Supplementary Reading:

James Kalat, *Introduction to Psychology*, 6th ed.

Questions to Consider:

1. Should psychology still be considered only one discipline, or should it be redefined into several disciplines?

2. Do you think the behaviorists were right—that it is ultimately impossible to know the inner workings of the human mind, or are the cognitive psychologists right—that there are ways of knowing the mind?

Lecture One—Transcript
Modern Psychology in Historical Context

Welcome to the Psychology of Human Behavior. I hope you enjoy this course. I am David Martin, and I am currently a professor of psychology at North Carolina State University. I have been teaching some form of survey of psychology for some 36 years. What we are going to do in this course is concentrate to a great extent on some modern advances in psychology, at the same time putting psychology within a historical context; so I hope you enjoy it. I find psychology to be the most interesting thing that there is—perhaps I am biased because I chose to be a psychologist—and I think you will find it interesting too. After all, if you go to a party and see what people are talking about, they are talking about other people and other people's behavior; "Why did she leave him?" "Why don't they bring up their kids in a better way?" They are talking about human behavior. So that is what we are going to be talking about in this course, and I think you will find it interesting. I certainly do.

What we are going to do today is, first of all, talk about what psychologists do, and make a distinction between psychologists and psychiatrists. Then we are going to talk about some of the precursors of psychology, particularly coming out of philosophy, but to some extent out of biology and out of physiology as well. Then we are going to talk some about the history of psychology; it is a fairly short history, over the 100 years or so. And then we are going to talk some about some of the major theoretical trends in psychology, both in experimental psychology and in clinical psychology.

Finally, we are going to do a quick look at the rest of the course and what we are going to do in those various lectures in the course, talk a little bit about what topics are included and why they are in the order that they are in this course. So that is our agenda for today.

What I do when I start my survey of psychology course is often ask students to picture a psychologist. Come up with a real image in your mind about a psychologist and what that psychologist might be doing. I then go around and pick on people and have them describe this person. What they typically come up with, at least on the first pass, is that they describe, it is usually a man; and it is a man usually with a beard, often with a German accent, sitting in a chair or taking notes, talking to a person lying on a couch, who is rambling on about their life and their childhood.

That is a good picture and it is a bad picture. It is a good picture in that it does in fact represent about two-thirds of the people who do psychology; that is, the general area of clinical psychology also including such things as counseling psychology and school psychology, to come up with that two-thirds figure. So it is a good picture in that respect.

However, it is also a bad picture in some respects, because indeed what they are probably describing is more like a psychiatrist than a psychologist to begin with. It is kind of an old fashioned setting, but it is one; in fact, they are probably describing Sigmund Freud, who we are going to talk about quite a bit in this course and some future lectures. It is kind of a bad picture that way. At least it gives you the idea of what many psychologists do. Many psychologists are trying to help people solve their problems. These are people who are having problems all the way from being fairly severely mentally ill to people who are maybe just having some problems in their life and looking for a more enriched life.

So those are clinical psychologists that do that; but what is the distinction between a clinical psychologist and a psychiatrist? The first distinction comes in terms of training. Psychiatrists tend to be medical doctors. They are trained as medical doctors: they go to school as a pre-med major as an undergraduate; they go on to school get a medical degree, dissect animals and that sort of thing, learn anatomy, and become a medical doctor. They then go on for a couple of more years of intensive psychotherapy, and in fact are psychoanalyzed themselves before they become psychiatrists. They then can prescribe medicine for you. They have drug prescription privileges. They can give you a physical examination, because they are medical doctors.

A clinical psychologist, on the other hand, has training usually as an undergraduate major in psychology, goes on to graduate school, gets a doctoral degree, usually a Ph.D. degree, which signifies a research degree so this person can do research if necessary. In some cases, they nowadays get a Psy.D degree, which is a doctor of psychology, which has a little less emphasis on research but they still have some training in research. This person cannot give you a physical exam, cannot prescribe drugs, although there is a current thing that is just starting to happen with prescription privileges for clinical psychologists, although it is still in its infancy. So, that is one of the major distinctions to make—in the clinical side—between a psychiatrist and a psychologist.

If I press them further and say, "Well, give me another picture." Many of them will come up with a picture of a fellow in a white lab coat; bald-headed fellow with glasses, with a rat under each arm, going down to the laboratory to run the rat in a maze. That again is a good picture and a bad picture. It is a good picture in that it does describe the folk who work in experimental psychology, which is the other one-third of the folks in psychology. It is a bad picture in that hardly any of these experimental psychologists today work on animals other than humans. Most of them work with humans. They are interested in people who are normal for the most part; so they are just interested in how people perceive things, how people remember things, how people learn things and what motivates people in all of these standard areas of psychology, many of which we are going to talk about in this course.

So that is the experimental psychologist. They may work in settings such as a laboratory, in a government operation, or perhaps, a laboratory in a university. And today, more and more often, they are also working in industrial organizational jobs in industry, or in ergonomics designing systems, that sort of thing.

Now, what I would like to do is move on and talk a little about the precursors of psychology, and most of these grew out of philosophy and to some extent biology. Let us go way back to the middle of the 1600s when Rene Descartes was speculating about the nature of the mind. And he was really the first one—at least he is given the credit—for being the one who made a distinction between the mind and the body, the mind being the idea of being innate and also being part of the self, and that is distinct from the body. So it is sort of the ghost within the machine notion that Rene Descartes came up with.

About fifty years later, John Locke came along and asserted that is not true at all; that there is no innate mind. He introduced the concept of *tabula rasa*, which means "blank slate." So his notion was that everything is blank and the slate is to be written on by our experiences. Through our sensory mechanisms, we bring in experiences and write on this blank slate. As we will see, much of psychology and the history of psychology is based upon this blank slate notion, and that is why Behaviorism, that we will talk about in a minute, became so prominent; because it was all having to do with learning, what was written on this blank slate.

David Hume came along about 1740, and he was a British associationist. He claimed that the mind is no more than a collection of sensory impressions that are linked together by associations. So the association of these things is what is important. This again, is sort of a precursor of Behaviorism as well. These associations are what happens when we do learning.

In the 1830s, Ernst Heinrich Weber was one of the empiricists. While he was not technically a psychologist, he was interested in studying mental and psychological operations in a quantitative way, especially on the sensory side of things—what our subjective experience is when we are presented with certain sensory stimuli— and he wanted to quantify this.

Charles Darwin came along around 1870 and proposed the theory of evolution, and we are going to talk a great deal about that in this course. The theory of evolution then put the human back in the animal kingdom again and said that indeed the human had certain kinds of built-in instincts, and we will deal with that in this course as well.

So those are kind of the precursors of psychology. This is all before psychology was identified as a separate field. Then in the late 1800s—the specific date 1879 is usually attributed to Wilhelm Wundt, who established the first psychological laboratory in the like of Germany—it was at this point that psychologists started to become empiricists and actually collect data and form a science.

In the late 1800s, William James, while not an empiricist himself— he did not collect data, but he read extensively about other people who did—and what William James did, he was a great writer and wrote a lot about psychology and really introduced it to America. Around the turn of century, around 1900, Sigmund Freud came along, and we will talk extensively about him. He was in Vienna, Austria, and most people associate him with clinical psychology. But he also introduced psychoanalytic theory, which is one of the major theories that is often cited in psychology, and introduced the unconscious mind as an important concept. Then, around 1910, Ivan Pavlov, who was a physiologist, discovered classical conditioning. This was sort of the beginning of the behaviorist era. We will talk about classical conditioning and have a whole lecture on classical conditioning later on in this course.

Around 1913, John Watson, who was an American, started the behaviorist movement and gave it its name, and he claimed that there are behaviors that should be studied; that we should not study the conscious mind; that all we can really study is behavior. B.F. Skinner, throughout the middle of the 1900s, also talked about the behaviorist tradition and introduced operant conditioning to most folks, which is a different form of learning. Again, we are going to talk about operant conditioning in this course.

Around the 1960s, Ulrich Neisser came along and introduced cognitive psychology. It is a different way of thinking about things. He said that you can measure things besides behavior, but, in fact, it is okay to look at the mind again, and that using fairly sophisticated techniques, we can understand what is going on in the mind. So they were measuring certain kinds of things, like reaction times, how long mental processes took, and inferring what the mind must be like if you get these kinds of measures. So this was the cognitive revolution, and it is a revolution which is still underway today. It is still the primary paradigm in psychology. However, around the 1990s, another paradigm has just started to be important in psychology, and it is based upon the mid-1970s work of E.O. Wilson, who published a book called *Social Biology* in the mid-1970s. This introduced people again to evolution, and perhaps indicated that evolution might be another way of looking at human behavior. It has had some very recent impact in psychology.

So that is kind of a quick history of the precursors of psychology, and then some of the major players in psychology over the last one hundred years. Now there have been several theoretical trends in psychology—I have already alluded to some of these as I was talking about the people—and some of these trends are in experimental psychology and some of these trends are in clinical psychology.

In experimental psychology around the turn of the century, shortly after the original laboratory was established for experimental psychology, the major way that people collected data was through what was called "introspection." People sat around—these were highly trained people; I do not mean to make too much light of it, but they were highly trained to be able to supposedly look into their own minds and figure out what the contents of the minds were. So they were trained so that a stimulus was presented to them, they would think about how they were processing that stimulus, how they processed the color, how they processed the form, and so forth. So they just thought about what was going on in their minds, and that was an approach to trying to discover what was going on in the human mind. The introspectionists lasted a few decades, but were fairly quickly knocked out by the behaviorists.

The behaviorists came along, people like I mentioned; like Pavlov and like Watson and later like Skinner, who came along and said that there is no way to know our own minds. How can we be both the thing doing the measuring and the thing being measured at the same time? That is an impossibility they said; there is no way that we can do that. So they said instead of doing that, we are going to measure the behavior. That is the only real subject matter for psychology, is to measure the behavior. Let us ignore what is going on in the mind since we do not have access directly to what is going on in the mind.

So they started to measure behavior; not only human behavior, in fact not very often human behavior, because they said that human behavior could be biased by in fact our conscious thinking, so we can change our behavior. So let us go study behavior of more basic organisms, like animals—like rats, like pigeons—and look at the behavior of these animals, which is simpler in nature and cannot sort of be overridden by conscious thought.

So this was sort of the heyday of the behaviorists. And indeed, in that area, perhaps the fellow with the rat under each arm going to the laboratory would have been an appropriate picture, because that is much of what went on during the behaviorist period; these people running animals and just measuring their behavior, looking at the behavior as it was influenced by things like whether or not that behavior was reinforced.

Behaviorists held sway for forty to sixty years in psychology, until the cognitive psychologists came along—I mentioned Neisser earlier—in the mid-1960s, and some things were happening that influenced psychology. Information processing and information theory came along. Computers came along, and people said: well we know something about computers; let's use the computer as a metaphor for what the human mind is like. We can figure out what goes on in a computer kind of the way the computer behaves—how long it takes the computer to do something by changing the input and looking at the output, and inferring what is going on. We can do the same sort of thing with the human mind. So it became legal again to look in the mind, but we did not have the person who was doing the thinking looking in his or her own mind. In this case, we had other people looking at the behavior and trying to infer what was going on in the mind. This was the cognitive revolution.

That revolution as I mentioned earlier, is still probably the predominant way that psychologists go about—especially experimental psychologists—their business. Although, there is this sort of new way of thinking from the evolutionary psychologists who claim that the mind is indeed not a blank slate. Even cognitive psychology is still looking at the mind to some extent as a blank slate; there is this big mainframe computer that in fact is written on, and as it is written on it gets its own software that is built into it. It still starts out kind of as a blank slate. They are no sort of modules and pieces to this computer. The evolutionary psychologists say, well maybe there are modules and pieces that come about through adaptations that were important from an evolutionary point of view. So that is a fairly recent trend in experimental psychology.

The clinical psychologists, on the other hand, were going about their own kind of set of revolutions. Freud, we already mentioned, around the turn of the century proposed that human motivations are largely at the unconscious level. And for this reason, it was required that highly trained psychoanalysts must spend many years trying to determine what is at the unconscious level in order to determine what their contents are, what the kind of conflict that is going on at the unconscious level, in order to correct these human problems.

Carl Rogers came along shortly after this, and he was a humanistic psychologist, and he proposed that well you do not really have to have a doctor up here and a patient down here with a big power differential, where the doctor knows how to cure the patient using a medical model. What he proposed is that we have a therapist and a client, and that these people are on fairly equal levels, and that the client has within himself or herself, some of the ability to solve their own problems. The therapist is just there to act kind of as a sounding board, to help this person solve the problems. It is not a directive the way psychoanalysis is, where you tell the patient what to do; in this case you allow the client to sort of seek his own way and get through the problems.

Behavior therapists came along slightly later after that. Along with the behaviorist revolution and experimental psychology, we had the behavior therapists suggesting that if you have problems, those problems may be the result of inappropriate learning; you have learned how to behave in the wrong way. So if we are going to intervene and try to correct those problems, the way to do that is to try to have the person relearn those behaviors; relearn appropriate behaviors instead. So the behavior therapists came along and used behaviorist techniques in order to try to help people solve problems, and that was kind of another revolution in clinical psychology.

Finally, as might be expected since we know the cognitive revolution occurred in experimental psychology, there was also a cognitive revolution in clinical psychology as well. The cognitive therapists came along and they said perhaps the problems people are having are due to inappropriate thought. That is, they are thinking the wrong thing; they are thinking negative thoughts, "Why did I do that? Why can't I ever get anything straight?" These people are causing themselves problems because of the way they are thinking about things. So our job, when we intervene and try to correct these problems, is to get people to think appropriate thoughts. So a great deal of what they do when they go into therapeutic sessions is teach people appropriate thoughts.

That is kind of the history of major movements in clinical psychology and experimental psychology. Now I would like to take a few minutes and talk about where we are going to in this course; what kind of topics we are going to cover and why we are covering them in the order that we are. After today's lecture, the next two lectures, Lectures Two and Three, are going to talk about the methodologies that are used in psychology. We are going to talk extensively in the next lecture about experimentation and why an experimental model is particularly important in the science of psychology and in science in general. Then in the next lecture we are going to talk about some other techniques that are used, like correlational observation; and some of the non-quantitative techniques, what are called qualitative methods that are used in psychology. And those are methods that are being used more and more frequently in psychology. We will deal some with those.

In Lecture Four we are going to look at evolutionary theory, just the very basics of evolutionary theory. I think it is important to do this early on because what I would like for you to do is think about evolutionary theory and sort of apply it to some of the standard concepts in psychology as we talk about those. We will come back later on and talk about evolutionary theory in a couple of lectures toward the end of the course. I think it is important to get some of the basics fairly early.

In Lectures Five and Six, we are going to talk about psychoanalytic theory that I have already talked about slightly today. This is Freud's theory of our personality. It is one of the major theories of personality. It has been important in the history of psychology, so we are going to talk about that some and some of the complexities of that theory. I think it is important to talk about that before we talk about the mental illnesses, because a lot of the mental illnesses we are going to talk about, classification systems for mental illnesses are based upon some of the basic notions in psychoanalytic theory.

In Lectures Seven through Eleven, we will talk about what makes abnormal behavior abnormal; why we think it is abnormal. And we will also talk about how we classify mental illnesses and use a very standard classification system for mental illnesses. So we'll talk about the various mental illnesses and sort of what goes into those mental illnesses; what some of the symptoms are.

In Lectures Twelve through Seventeen, we are going to consider several categories of therapies. We talk about therapies, in this case, kind of separate from the mental illnesses. You might think it would be better to talk about the mental illness and then immediately talk about the therapy—sort of like if you have appendicitis, what do you do to correct appendicitis—but in psychology, rather strangely I think, therapy is often determined more by the training of the therapist than it is by the particular mental illness. We have therapists that are behavior therapists and that is largely what they do; who are psychoanalysts and that is largely what they do. They will bring this therapy to bear on a number of different classifications of mental illness. So we are going to talk about those three categories of therapy, including physical kinds of therapies, where we intervene with drugs or with psychosurgery or with genetic engineering; therapies that are behavior therapies, that are based upon learning; and therapies that are the more traditional therapies, such as the talking therapies, like psychoanalysis and cognitive therapies and some of those kinds of the therapies.

In Lectures Eighteen through Twenty-Two, we are going to look at some theories of motivation and emphasize in particular the homeostatic model that is kind of a physiological theory of motivation. We will also talk about emotion to some extent, and emphasize how difficult it is even to measure emotions since it is a private event within us. We will also talk some about psychoactive drugs, because psychoactive drugs have a major impact on emotions.

In Lectures Twenty-Three through Twenty-Four, we will look in detail at influence. Influence is one of the sub-topics of social psychology, and influence—we don't have time to cover all of social psychology—so influence, I think, is one of the more interesting ones; and I hope you take some practical notions away from this about how to influence other people.

In Lectures Twenty-Five through Thirty-One, we are going to explore three of the major research areas of experimental psychology. These are learning, memory and perception. We are going to emphasize some modern advances that have been made in these areas. There is a whole new notion about constructive processes and how important these are in those three areas. So we are going to talk about learning and how we go about learning, both in a historical context and a more modern context. We will talk about memory and we will talk about perception.

In Lectures Thirty-Three through Thirty-Four, we will talk about evolutionary psychology in more detail, because evolutionary psychology, in my opinion, is a theory that gives us sort of an overarching approach to psychology, and brings psychology back into the whole scientific realm of biology and some of the other sciences. I think it is an important advancement that we are making, and also allows us to ask some questions that drew us into an interest in psychology in the first place. We are interested in psychology often because of being able to answer "why" questions. Why did she do that? Why did he do that? Why did this happen or that happen in terms of human behavior? Much of psychology up to this point has been asking not "why" questions, but "how" and "what" questions. What did this person do in this circumstance? Not, why did this person do it. Part of the reason for this is that we have not had an overarching theory. What evolutionary psychology does is give us a chance to look at these behaviors and ask why questions, the most interesting questions, I think, in psychology.

In Lecture Thirty-Five we are going to consider engineering psychology, probably a topic you have never even heard of. I was actually trained as an engineering psychologist, so I want to give at least one lecture on this. Engineering psychology is also sometimes called human factors or ergonomics, and it allows us to look at the human as an operator of a human machine system. It exemplifies a whole area of applied psychology. So, I think it is important that we look at at least one of the areas of applied psychology.

In Lecture Thirty-Six we are going to do a quick review of where we have been and what we have covered in the course. We will give a bit of a thumbnail sketch to some areas that we have not had time to cover; for example developmental psychology, and in particular gerontology, the study of older people. We will look some at cognitive modeling and what cognitive modeling can do. We will also look some at neuropsychology and the workings of the brain just very briefly in this final lecture.

So, that is where we are going to go. Today what we have done is just give you a quick overview. We talked a little bit about what psychologists do, and the distinction between the psychologist and a psychiatrist. We looked some about some of the precursors of psychology and how they have influenced psychology coming from philosophy; things like the *tabula rasa*, the mind and how to study the mind, associationists. Then we looked at some of the interesting folks in psychiatry during the history of psychology, and some of the major theoretical trends in psychology as well, and how the early philosophers influenced them.

Finally, we looked about where we are going in this course; and that is where we are going to go and I hope you enjoy it as we do that. Thank you for your attention.

Lecture Two
Experimentation as a Research Method

Scope:

Experimentation has been adopted as one of the primary research methods of psychology. In an experiment, there is an attempt to establish a causal relationship between at least one circumstance and one behavior. Of the infinite number of circumstances, one circumstance, called the *independent variable*, is operationally defined by the experimenter and set on at least two levels. A behavior is then operationally defined and measured as the independent variable is manipulated. Other circumstances, called *control variables*, are set and not allowed to vary during the experiment. Some circumstances, are allowed to vary by chance; in an experiment, these are called *random variables*. Random variables contribute to the generalizability of results. Well-designed experiments have no *confounding variables*, which are those that change along with the levels of the independent variable.

Outline

I. As a science, much of psychology has modeled itself after the so-called hard sciences and adopted experimentation as a primary research methodology.

   A. Suppose you were asked to pretend you were a psychologist conducting research on the question: "Does violence on TV cause aggression in children?"

      1. Many people would propose doing an experiment that involved at least two groups of children, one that watched violent TV shows and one that watched nonviolent TV shows.

      2. An immediate problem is how to define *violent* with respect to TV shows.

      3. What is required is an operational definition that describes the operations one would go through to determine which shows are violent and which are nonviolent (for example, ratings systems, checklists, and so on).

B. Another problem is to determine how to measure aggression in children.

   1. Saying that we will observe the children's behavior is not enough.

   2. Again, what is required is an operational definition of aggression, such as the percent of time the children play with aggressive versus nonaggressive toys.

C. Another problem is choosing representative children to use in the groups.

   1. Should children be randomly assigned, or should they be chosen to represent some established criteria?

   2. Randomization is a powerful selection mechanism that can eliminate the need to control many variables.

II. Experimentation is an agreed-on way to establish a causal relationship between a circumstance and a behavior.

A. Picture on the left a vertical list of individual circumstances that we want to relate to one or more behaviors.

   1. For our thought experiment, the list might include such items as violent TV shows, size of TV set, age of children, size of group watching TV, length of time in each TV session, number of TV sessions, and so on.

   2. This list would be potentially infinite in length.

B. To indicate the possible behaviors that could be measured, picture a vertical list on the right that shows all behaviors that could possibly be measured.

   1. For our thought experiment, the list might include such items as type of toys played with, number of hitting incidents, noise level of the room, and so on.

   2. The list of behaviors is also potentially infinite.

C. Imagine an arrow pointing from the list of circumstances to the list of behaviors, indicating that the purpose of any experiment is to establish a causal relationship between circumstances and behaviors.

III. When conducting an experiment, some choices must be made regarding the circumstances and the behaviors.

  A. First, at least one of the circumstances must be chosen to manipulate, that is, to be set on at least two levels.

  1. The circumstance that the experimenter chooses to manipulate is called the *independent variable* because it is independent of the subject's behavior.

  2. In our thought experiment, the independent variable would be something like viewing violent TV shows versus viewing nonviolent TV shows.

  B. At least one behavior must also be chosen to be measured during the experiment.

  1. The behavior that the experimenter chooses to measure is called the *dependent variable* because it is potentially dependent on the levels of the independent variable.

  2. In our thought experiment, the dependent variable might be time spent playing with aggressive toys or nonaggressive toys, as defined by the operational definition.

  C. Although the rest of the items on the behavior list can now be ignored, the rest of the circumstances list must be partitioned.

  1. Some of the circumstances must be set at a particular level and not be allowed to vary during the experiment; these are called *control variables* because the experimenter exerts control over them.

  2. In our thought experiment, some control variables might be size of the TV viewing group, size of the TV set, size of the TV viewing room, external noise allowed into the room, and so on.

  3. Some of the circumstances will be allowed to vary through random selection; these are called *random variables*.

  4. In our experiment, some random variables might include the children's socioeconomic status, the day of the week, or the weather outside.

  5. Random variables are necessary in some cases because it is impossible to control some circumstances.

6. Random variables are also desirable in some cases because they allow results to be generalized to a larger population.

D. Experimenters must avoid having one or more circumstances vary along with the levels of the independent variable.

    1. When a circumstance varies along with the independent variable, it is called a *confounding variable.*

    2. A confounding variable makes the results of an experiment ambiguous because it is not possible to know whether the change in behavior was the result of the independent variable or the confounding variable.

    3. In our thought experiment, if one group watched 2 hours of nonviolent TV and the other group watched 4 hours of violent TV, we wouldn't know whether any change in aggressiveness was the result of violence or time spent watching.

IV. Another example is an experiment I conducted that attempted to measure the relationship between students' attentiveness and the professor's lecture pace.

A. I varied the lecture pace from slow to medium to fast.

B. Ambient noise levels in the lecture room were measured.

C. The idea behind this was that when the students were quieter, they were more attentive; when they were rustling papers and talking, they were less attentive.

D. Graphing the noise level as a function of low, medium, and high pace, I found that the students were most attentive when I spoke at a medium pace.

E. This experiment embodied potential confounding variables.

    1. My voice pitch tended to get lower when I spoke at a slower pace and higher when I spoke at a faster pace.

    2. The number of words I used to talk about a concept also varied, depending on the pace of my speech.

    3. It is important to be aware of confounding variables to try to eliminate them or, if that is not possible, to explain them.

V. If you manipulate an independent variable, measure a dependent variable, manage your controlled and random variables, and have no confounding variables, then you can attribute the change in behavior to the levels of the independent variables. This is a causal statement; the change in the independent variable caused the change in the dependent variable. This is the only methodology we have in which one piece of research shows a causal relationship between a set of circumstances and behavior.

Essential Reading:

David Martin, *Doing Psychology Experiments*, 6th ed., chapter 2.

Supplementary Reading:

Keith Stanovich, *How to Think Straight about Psychology*, 7th ed.

Questions to Consider:

1. What would be good operational definitions for the following terms: *intelligence, spousal abuse, attention*?

2. Under what conditions is randomization preferable to control in an experiment?

Lecture Two—Transcript
Experimentation as a Research Method

This is the first of two lectures on the methods that are used in psychology to investigate human behavior. These methods include quantitative methods—that from which you get data that add up into numbers and for which you can do statistics; but also qualitative methods, where the data are not quite so clear.

So, we are going to talk about both of those over this two-lecture series. Today it is going to be specifically on experimentation, which is definitely a quantitative method in psychology. But first I would like to step back a minute and ask the question whether psychology is indeed a science, because we are claiming to use scientific methodologies here. When I ask my students that, sometimes—and I teach in a university where we have a lot of engineers and a lot of hard scientists—and they sort of get a smirk on their face and say, "Well, psychology can never be a legitimate science after all. How can you possibly predict an individual's behavior? You cannot do that. I can predict the behavior of a block on an inclined plane," Or the chemists say, "When we add two chemicals together I can predict the behavior. You can never predict the behavior of an individual. So how are you going to do that? How is this ever going to be a science?"

Then I try to convince them that indeed we can look at human behavior. It is true that for a single individual we cannot predict their behavior except in a probabilistic sense; we can predict it that way. We cannot determine deterministically, say, how the person is going to behave. But you will discover in some of the other sciences, with chaos theory and other kinds of theories, they cannot exactly predict what the state of that atom is going to be either, except in a probabilistic sense. Nobody accuses the physicists of not being scientific.

So, I like to try to convince them that in fact psychology is the most sophisticated of the sciences because we do have to deal with human variability in what we do. Much of what I am going to talk about today will be experimental method is dealing somehow with variability in the sort of more naturalistic setting that psychologists have to work with, rather than the setting that the hard scientist—so called hard scientists—have to deal with. Psychology has come up with some very sophisticated statistical ways of dealing with its variability as well.

What is a science exactly? Well it is some—if you ask people that, most of them say, well it is kind of a collection of facts. That is true. It is kind of a more organized collection of facts, and those facts are usually a relationship between variables. Usually that relationship is between a set of circumstances and a particular behavior. If you are a chemist, you want to know the circumstances of putting this chemical at this particular temperature and this particular purity in with another chemical, and what happens; what is the behavior when that happens. If you are a physicist you might want to know you have this block on an inclined plane; and at a particular angle and a particular surface on the plane, a particular mass of the block, what is the behavior? What is the relationship of that set of circumstances to behaviors?

In psychology we are no different. We are just looking at human behavior and we are trying to say, "What are the circumstances that lead to a particular behavior?" The best kind of statement we can make is not only that the circumstances are related to the behavior, but in fact, the circumstances cause the behavior. The nice thing about experimentation that we are going to spend this lecture talking about is the fact that it is one of the scientific methods that can be used to say one thing caused something else. I hope I convince you of that today. It is a very powerful kind of tool, experimentation is. Not the only tool in science, as we will see; it is difficult, for example, for an astronomer to do experimentation. You cannot move this planet from here to here to see what happens. So very often they cannot do experiments. They can do little experiments, but typically they cannot do the big experiments that would be necessary.

So there are other techniques in science, and we are going to talk about some of those other techniques in the next lecture. Today, we want to talk about experimentation. Now when I do this in my class, what I typically do is say, "Okay, in order to understand experimentation, I think the best way is for me to make you an experimental psychologist. So I hereby declare that you are an experimental psychologist." Now, pretend I work for the government and I have millions of dollars to solve a particular behavior problem.

What I want you to do is propose a way of solving this problem. You are now a researcher and I want you to solve this problem. The question is: does violence on television cause aggression in children? That is actually kind of an old problem in psychology this has been studied for some forty or so years in psychology. But pretend this is the first time you ever heard it. Does violence on television cause aggression in children? I do not want your opinion about this and I do not want you to collect other people's opinion about this. What I want you to do is figure out a way of doing some research, collecting some data that will help convince me that yes it does or no it does not; because what the government wants, of course, is I got this money from the legislature, and they want to go back and look at Saturday morning programs for kids and they want to look at what kids are watching on television and they are concerned about shootings in schools and things like that. So, they want to know whether the violence on television is a contributing factor to this kind of behavior. That is the purpose of this kind of thing.

I want you to sit and think about this problem and come up with a solution; that is what I tell my students, and then I give them five minutes or so to do this rather artificial situation and they talk amongst themselves. Then I say, "Okay what have you come up with? What kinds of research are you going to do?" I will tell you some of the general kind of research they suggest. "Well, Dr. Martin what we are going to do is we are going to go out and sample a whole bunch of kids and bring them in and have them watch television shows. They are going to sit and watch the television show for an hour a day and we will do this for about a month and then we will observe their behavior. One group of kids is going to watch violent television and come in and watch that an hour a day for a month, and the other group will come in and watch nonviolent television for an hour a day for a month. And then we are going to put them in a room and we are going to observe them and see who is more aggressive, and that is our solution." That is the typical situation that the student comes up with.

Now that is good in some respects. They have created an experiment indeed. They have all of the requirements for that experiment, at least superficially. But in some respects they have not dealt with a whole lot of questions that you need to deal with before you do an experiment. So let us talk about some of those questions. I ask them,

"Well you just said that you are going to show them violent television shows. What does that mean? How do you know violence on television when you see it?" "Well we know some shows are violent. I mean, *CSI* is violent maybe, and the shoot 'em up kind of shows are violent, and I know that when I see it. We will just pick up the violent ones and the nonviolent ones." I'll say, "Well that is not quite good enough." You see, if somebody wanted to repeat this experiment some time in the future or validate it to see whether you did it right, they would have to know how you defined violence on television so they can define it the same way. In fact what they need is what is called an "operational definition" of violence.

What operations would you go through to try to define violence? Well let us see. How about—let us make a list of things that are violent. If somebody hits somebody else, that is violent. Okay, we will write than down on the list. That is part of our definition, if somebody hit somebody else. If somebody insults somebody else, that is violence. Okay, we will write that. If there is blood involved that is violence. Okay we will write that down. If death is involved, that is violence. Okay we will write that. So we can write down a whole big, long list and operational define violence that way; and every time you saw a television show, go over that list to see how many of those—maybe you need four out of the ten things on the list to make it a violent show. That would be an operational definition.

However, there is still some subjective judgment involved in terms of looking at the show and trying to decide whether the list was appropriate. And there might be some question about some of the things; for example, NFL Football. Is that violent? People hit each other, do not they? Blood is involved sometimes, right? So we can check that off. But is it really violence? It is certainly violence within a very socially accepted version of violence, and these people are allowed to behave this way and not scorned. In fact they are rewarded, quite nicely, for behaving this way. What about *Roadrunner* cartoons? You got Wile E. Coyote chasing the Roadrunner around off a cliff and that sort of thing. People, they never seem to die for some reason after falling off these big cliffs, but there is certainly a lot of hitting and violence involved in that. But these are not really humans either, are they? In fact the whole point is humor and not a more serious kind of point. So, there may be problems with this. Another way that they can operational define it is to bring together, say, a group of 100 people that you would pick. You would show them ten minutes of one of these shows and then have them rate the show; just use their human judgment, whatever their internal definition of violence is. If this is a 10, it is the most violent thing you have ever seen, and if this is a zero, that is the least violent thing that you have ever seen. And we can operational define it that way.

At least that way the next person could do the same thing—bring together another group of one hundred people, show them the television show and have them rate it in much the same manner. So that is at least a nice operational definition that way. So, you have to be kind of careful what you are doing when you look at violence, but you have to be careful on the aggression side too. These people kind of blithely said, "Well we are going to observe them and see how aggressive they are." Well how do you define aggression? It is the same kind of problem. You need an operational definition. And again, you could make up the list: whenever Johnny hit Susie that is aggression; if Johnny is saying nasty things to Susie that is aggression and so forth. So we could make another list up that way. What they want to do, of course, is to hire a psychologist to tell then whether or not it is aggressive behavior, but psychologists do not have any magic answers either to these kinds of things.

So, there are a number of ways you could measure this. A way often suggested, taking a group of toys; and we will have aggressive toys and non-aggressive toys. So in aggressive toys we got play guns and play knives and tanks and that sort of thing, and the non-aggressive toys we got dolls and we got trucks and we got tractors and we got those kind of things. So we will put out these toys and let them pick and choose what they are going to play with, and see whether they play with the aggressive toys or the non-aggressive toys. Sounds like a good idea perhaps, although one might be able to argue that they are just imitating, and if they just saw a violent television show with guns and knives, they know how to use those. Maybe they do not really know quite how to use the truck and the tractor as well if they are watching non-violence. So maybe they are just imitating; they are not really being aggressive as they do this. So there may be problems with it, but at least that would give us a nice quantitative measure of behavior. We could argue one way or another whether the operational definition is a good one.

Also, one of the problems is how do you know a representative sample when you get one? These people are concerned with—the students are—because they often say, "Well we want to make sure that we get people from different socio-economic classes. We want to make sure we get people from different amounts of violence in the home or aggression in the home; from different ethnic groups and so forth." So we want a representative group somehow. But they do not know quite how to do that; whether they can randomize it or whether they can do something else. So that is also a concern that often comes up here.

So that is what they do in this little exercise I give them. And what I would like to do now is go to kind of a model of an experiment and see how this little exercise we just did fits into that model. And this model will allow us to look at causal relationships, because it is an experiment. Imagine on the left that we have a whole list of circumstances that we might be able to vary; and those circumstances can be all sorts of things, anything that they might go into this kind of experiment. Now we know one that is going to go in there, and that is violence versus non-violence, because that is part of our question. So we know we want that to be a particular circumstance. But there are other circumstances as well that we have to decide on, and what to do with those circumstances; things like what size television set are we going to use? Or, what is the children's age that we are going to use? What is the group size; how many kids are we going to have watching this television set? What is the room size? How many sessions are we going to have? What is the length of a session? How much television are they going to watch? What day of the week? What is the socio-economic status of the kids, and so forth?

We could make a list, essentially, of an infinite list of circumstances over on the left side. What we want to do remember with science is relate the circumstances to behaviors. So over on the other side we have all sorts of behaviors that we could potentially measure. Now in our case, since the question had to do with aggression, we would know kind of what we would want to measure; things like what toys do they play with, or something like that. But there are all sorts of other behaviors that are going on here as well, such as how many hitting incidents there are, what the noise in the rooms is, how often they go to the bathroom. We could measure all sorts of different kinds of things, but all behaviors on the behavior side. What we want to do with our science is relate this set of circumstances on the left side to the behaviors on the right side. And we can draw an arrow across to indicate that is the rule or the law that we are looking for; that is the relationship, and it would be a causal relationship between the circumstances and behaviors.

Now, in order to turn this into an experiment, we need to partition out the circumstances and pick a behavior. So let us pick a circumstance of interest, that has already been picked by our question, violence on television; and the folks I ask this—even though they were not professional psychologists—knew sort of immediately that they had to have at least two levels of that. So they have to have violent television and nonviolent television, minimally. They could have other levels as well; they could have a kind of a neutral level or they could have a no television level or they could have other kinds of levels as well, but they have to have at least two. After all, if I just showed you violent television and had no other group and measure the behavior, I would say, "Oh, these people are pretty aggressive. It must be due to the violent television." You could rightly come to me and say, "How do you know?" Maybe they would be just as aggressive if they had never seen your television show and you would be absolutely right. So we know we have to have at least two levels. Sometimes those are called the "control group" or the "control level" and the "experimental group." Now those are useful sometimes when you have a particular treatment, but in this case, just have violent versus nonviolent, it really doesn't make much sense to call one a control group and one an experimental group. But we need two levels.

So we pick that and manipulate that and we call that the "independent variable." So the circumstance we pick to manipulate at least two levels is called the independent variables. It is call independent variable because it is independent of anything that the subject or the participant might do in the experiment. They cannot come in and say, "I want to watch the violent television," because we assign them to that. They do not have any choice over it. It is independent of its own behavior. On the other side, we have to pick at least one behavior to measure. We already talked about that a little bit—the proportion of toys that they play with, the number of hitting incidents, or what exactly are we going to measure; let us assume that we have at least operationally defined it and picked one behavior. That is called the "dependent variable." The dependent variable is called that because it is ostensibly dependent upon the levels of the independent variable. Okay? So we have now picked the dependent variable as well. On the behavior side we can ignore the other behaviors essentially. We cannot do that on the circumstances side. We have all of these other circumstances here that we cannot just ignore. So what are we going to do with those circumstances? What immediately comes to mind for most people are, well, let us set them at a particular level and not allow them to vary. All right, so they are all going to watch the same size television set. They are all going to watch it in the same size group, say six kids watching it, in the same size room at the same time of day. Let us just set everything else and make them all what are called "control variables." A control variable is a variable you set at a particular level and you do not allow it to vary during the experiment.

Indeed, that is what is done for the most part in the hard sciences. They set up lots of control variables; so the chemist wants to make sure the temperature is the same and the purity is the same and the particular composition is the same. They set up lots of control variables. We set up some control variables in psychology, but there is a problem. The first problem is we could not possibly set all of them up as control variables. For example, there are differences between the kids, right? We are not allowed to clone kids for experiments. You might like to do that, but we cannot do it; and so we have to get what we can take in terms of kids. We cannot say, "Okay, the weather is going to perfect for all of these experiments." The weather changes and there is nothing we can do about it. Lots of different kinds of things change that we do not have much control over. So we cannot set up everything as a control variable and frankly we would not want to if we could because if we set everything up as a control variable, we would not be able to generalize our results to anything. Suppose we could set everything up and so we set up this experiment and we picked only kids in St. Louis, from a particular community in St. Louis, whose parents make between $30,000 and $32,000 a year, who are from a particular ethnic group who in all of the control variables that we have set a particular level. Then we finish our experiment and I said, "I've got your answer for you. Violence on television causes aggression in kids." And somebody might say, "Well that is great! Can we go use this?" And you say, "Wait a minute. It only works in St. Louis from kids from this community whose parents make this amount of money." Wait a minute. That is not what I wanted to know. I wanted to know, in general, does violence in television cause aggression in kids? So you couldn't generalize it to the whole population you are interested in. And that is why you do not want to make everything into a control variable, even if you could.

Another option is to make it into a random variable. And random variables save psychologist's career, because a random variable you just—as long as you do things in a random fashion, and that is not always easy—you have to make sure it is a random fashion. If you are picking the group of kids to use, you have to put all the names in a hat and draw them out individually, or at least do so maybe on a computer where you put all the names in there and randomly pick them out. Then you hope that randomization works; and it usually does, for larger numbers at least. Suppose we are using 100 kids here and you pick one for the violent television group and one for the nonviolent television group. You would expect that on average you are not going to get all of them in the violent group coming from highly aggressive homes for example, with highly punitive behavior, let us say, and all of the ones in the other group from non-aggressive homes. On average, they are going to have about the same number, and they are going to come from about the same socioeconomic class, about the same ethnicity, if it is truly randomly selected.

So a number of these variables we can partition and call random variables, and that gives us a lot of power; not quite as much precision, but it give us the ability to generalize to other populations. A variable we want to be very careful about, because what is called a "confounding variable"; we do not want any of our circumstances to come up to be confounding variables. Confounding variable is a variable that changes along with the levels of the independent variable, usually accidentally. We usually do not know that is happening. And that may not make much sense. Let me illustrate it within our situation. Suppose you were running the violent television group and the nonviolent television group, and you looked around for television shows, and the way you defined it, you had a dickens of a time finding anything that was nonviolent, because in fact most television shows are fairly violent. In fact, all you can find for your month-long experiment, if you are showing television to the kids every day, is about four hours of violent television; but you can only find two hours of nonviolent television. So you set up your experiment that way. You run four hours of violent television, and the nonviolent folks watch only two hours. You do your experiment and you find that violence on television causes aggression in children and you say that is our conclusion you write it up in the report. Somebody could step in very easily and say, "Now wait a minute, Dr. Martin. I do not think you showed that at all. I think what you showed was that the more television they watched the more aggressive they are, and it is four hours versus two hours rather than violent versus nonviolent." And they would be absolutely right. I would have no defense against that. I would say, "Okay, you are right it could be that." That would have sort of killed my experiment, wouldn't it?

Now I probably would not be quite so stupid as that. Suppose instead that I did show four hours to each of the groups and I write up my report and my lab assistant comes in when this is done and says, "You know, Dr. Martin, you were not there. I was there while they were watching television, and those kids watching the violent television, boy were they engrossed in that television show. Probably 80% of the time their eyes were on that television set; they thought it was great. I watched the kids watching the nonviolent show too, and they probably were not making eye contact more than 20% of the time with the television. They were off doing something else most of the time. That bored them to death." So in fact one group was watching a lot more television than the other group. And I said, "Uh, I cannot believe we let that happen. We have got a confounding variable here, don't we? You go back in there and make those kids watch the television show. Every time they turn away, you yell at them, slap them upside the head, you do whatever is necessary to get them to watch that television show." And then we run the experiment, and you can imagine how it is going to come out now. Probably the nonviolent group is going to be more aggressive than the other group because of all the pressure we put on them. You see what the problem is—we have a confounding variable again in there. And in real world experiments, it is sometimes very difficult to get rid of confounding variables.

Let me give you another example of another confounding variable from a real experiment I did a number of years ago. A graduate student in educational psychology and I decided to do an experiment looking at lecture pace and looking at attentiveness of students as a function of lecture pace for my class. I had a class of about 200 Introduction to Psychology students out there, sitting at tables in chairs, taking notes. And I would come in, and some days I would lecture at a very slow pace, much like this, where I had lots of spaces between my words. They thought I was hungover when I did this, but nevertheless I did this. I came in some days and for a 10-minute period of time I would lecture at a fairly medium pace much like I am doing now. And some days I would come in and just go gangbusters, just talking about like I am now, and I do that again for 10 minutes. And we would measure my pace and measure the number of syllables per minute to make sure I was producing the right pace. Then we would measure ambient noise level of the student in the room. We measured some other things as well, but one of the more important ones we measured ambient noise level and subtracted out my particular noise that I was making up there at the podium. When they are more attentive, the idea is they are quieter. When they are not being attentive, they are rustling around their papers, dropping their pencils and talking to each other and that sort of thing, so we measured the ambient noise level.

What we found, and reported in the literature in fact, if you graph noise level as a function of low, medium, and high pace, we found kind of a "V" shaped function, and that is good. Because what is says is they are most attentive when I am speaking at a medium pace. When I am speaking at the low pace, they make more noise; if I am speaking at the high pace, they make more noise. So that was kind of a good result we got. We were proud of that and it was reported in the literature. I might point out that there are potential confounding variables in that. When I speak at a low pace, much like most people, my voice is fairly low. As I speak a little faster, the tone of my voice, the fundamental frequency goes up and when I speak fast my voice is way up here. So in fact, if you wanted to plot along the bottom instead of low, medium, and fast paced, you could plot low, medium, and high fundamental frequency of my voice. There is no way, short of recording it and speech clipping, and doing some other kinds of things which would be very artificial, to make it go any other way. So naturally I had a confounding variable.

I also had a confounding variable in terms of how many words I used to talk about a concept. Either I would make the concepts come quicker, or I would use more words to talk about the same concept. So one of those had to naturally vary, and that was another confounding variable. So when you do real world experiments, like violence on television, you often get naturally occurring confounding variables. It is very important to realize that there are confounding variables, if there are, and be able to have alternative explanations for those confounding variables.

Now I might point out again, as I did early on here, that the real beauty of experimentation here is the fact that you can make a causal statement. We just all agreed in science that if you do manipulate an independent variable where the experimenter manipulates it, and you do not let the participant mess with your independent variable, and measure a dependent variable, and you do control your control variables and you do legitimately randomize your random variables, and you do not have a confounding variable if you follow all those rules, then we agree in science that you can attribute the change in behavior to the levels of the independent variable, a very powerful thing. A causal statement—and it is kind of an agreement that we all have—it seems to work—is the main reason we can agree that is the case. So this is the only real technique we have where one piece of research will show a causal relationship between a set of circumstances and behaviors, and that makes it a very powerful technique for methodologies in psychology.

Next time we will talk about some techniques that are not quite so powerful but are also used in psychology. Thank you.

Lecture Three
Nonexperimental Research Methods

Scope:

After experimentation, the next most widely used research method in psychology is *correlational observation*, in which there is no independent variable. In this case, the researcher attempts to determine whether there is a relationship between two behaviors. A statistical test can provide a correlation coefficient, which can indicate a strong relationship (the closer it is to 1.0) or a weaker relationship (the closer it is to 0). The numerical sign signifies the direction of the relationship. A single correlational observation cannot be used to infer causality, because we cannot determine which variable caused the other variable to change or if some third variable caused both to change. Psychologists also sometimes use qualitative designs to do research: *ethnography*, which is used to find behavior patterns through interviews and observation; *naturalistic observation*, in which behavior is observed in its natural setting; and *case studies*, in which a single individual is studied extensively and usually over a period of time to reveal recurring patterns. Qualitative designs have a number of limiting factors, including inability to draw causal inferences, limits on the use of statistical tests, subjectivity, and reliance on memory.

Outline

I. The second most widely used research method in psychology is *correlational observation*.

   A. When correlational observation is used, no independent variable is manipulated.

   1. In correlational observation, the researcher attempts to determine whether there is a relationship between two behaviors that are usually both under the control of the subject.

   2. If we were trying to relate viewing violence on TV to aggression in children, we might have parents keep a TV log to determine the average level of violence of the shows watched and ask teachers to rate the aggressiveness of each child.

B. To determine whether there was a relationship between violence and aggression, a statistical computation could be used to find the correlation coefficient.

    1. A correlation coefficient of 1.0 indicates that one variable is perfectly predictable from the other.

    2. A correlation coefficient of 0 indicates that neither variable is useful in predicting the other one.

    3. A correlation coefficient with a + sign indicates that as one variable increases, the other increases; a − sign indicates that as one variable increases, the other decreases.

C. Because no variable is independently manipulated, a single correlational observation cannot be used to establish causality.

    1. In our TV research, even if we found a strong relationship between the average level of violence viewed on TV and the children's aggressiveness, we could not conclude that the TV viewing caused the aggressiveness.

    2. One reason for our inability to establish causality is that, although the first variable might have caused the change in the second variable, alternatively, the second variable might have caused the change in the first. This is a problem of *directionality.*

    3. For example, in our TV research, it may be that aggressive children choose to watch TV shows having more violence.

    4. A second reason for our inability to infer causality is that a third variable that we haven't even measured might have unknowingly caused the relationship between the ones we measured.

    5. In our TV research, perhaps aggressive parents teach their children to be aggressive and aggressive parents also pick more violent TV shows for their children to watch.

D. An additional example illustrating the difficulty in inferring causality from correlational data is an experiment that attempted to predict G.I. motorcycle accidents.

1. It was found that the more tattoos a G.I. had, the more motorcycle accidents he had.

2. Clearly, motorcycle accidents do not cause tattoos, nor do tattoos cause motorcycle accidents.

3. The tattoos and motorcycle accidents are probably related through a third variable, such as a preference for bodily risk.

E. Cigarette packs make a causal statement—that smoking causes health problems.

1. We knew many years ago that people who smoke have more health problems—a correlational observation.

2. But we can't make a causal statement from a correlational observation, and it was not until all other possible third variables were eliminated as possible causes through additional research that a causal statement could be made.

F. Surveys are usually done with correlational data—no independent variables have been manipulated. Surveys have the advantage of access to opinions, but because the data are correlational, we can't make causal statements from them.

G. We should also be wary of news headlines, which often make causal statements from correlational observations.

II. Experimentation and correlational observation are both considered quantitative research designs because the data collected are numerical, but qualitative designs are sometimes used in psychology, in which the data cannot be quantified.

A. *Ethnography* attempts to observe and collect data from those living in a particular culture or undergoing a common experience.

1. Ethnographers may interview individuals to understand common patterns of behavior.

2. Ethnographers sometimes set up focus groups that bring together individuals who have similar life experiences.

B. In *naturalistic observation*, behaviors are observed within their naturally occurring setting by an unobtrusive observer.

C. In *case-history research* (also called *case studies*) the behavior of a single individual is studied extensively and usually over a period of time in order to reveal recurring patterns.

D. Care must be taken in drawing conclusions from qualitative research.

    1. Inferring causation is particularly dangerous because the data are correlational and, thus, no variable has been independently manipulated.

    2. Most qualitative research does not lend itself to the standard statistical techniques used in quantitative research.

    3. Interpretations of behaviors are typically more subjective and open to researcher biases.

    4. Case-history research has the additional drawback of being based on data that may be subject to memory loss or distortion.

Essential Reading:

David Martin, *Doing Psychology Experiments*, 6th ed., chapter 1.

Supplementary Reading:

John Creswell, *Research Design: Qualitative, Quantitative, and Mixed Methods Approaches*, 2nd ed., chapter 10.

W. R. Shadish, T. D. Cook, and D. T. Campbell, *Experimental and Quasi-experimental Designs for Generalized Causal Inference*.

Questions to Consider:

1. Can you think of a case where there would likely be a strong correlational relationship between two variables without a causal relationship?

2. Why do you think it took so long for a statement to be printed on the outside of cigarette packs warning that, in one way or another, smoking causes health problems?

Lecture Three—Transcript
Nonexperimental Research Methods

This is the second lecture in a two lecture series, "Methodologies in Psychology." You may recall that in our last lecture we talked extensively about experimentation and the experiment as a major tool for psychology and for science in general. We said that one of the real advantages of experimentation was that it allowed a causal statement to be made; that you could manipulate an independent variable, measure a dependent variable, and make a causal statement—that it was the independent variable that caused the change in the dependent variable. That is a very nice and a very powerful thing to be able to do. However, there are those who think that experimentation, particularly in psychology, has its problems.

One of the problems is how artificial it is. You remember we were talking about, "Does violence on television cause aggression in children?" What we did was take children and haul them into the laboratory and set them down in front of a television set with five other children to watch this television, and then we put them together to observe their behavior after that. Pretty artificial. That is not the way they watch television at home. They, in fact, get a chance to choose their own television often at home, or at least their parents do; and then they sit there and they wander in and out of the room and sit down and change channels and all sorts of other different kinds of natural things happening. To put them in this experimental context and constrain it the way we do, some people would say that it is pretty difficult to generalize from those kinds of experiments to the real life situation that is far more natural.

So that is one of the criticisms of experimentation, even though it is a very powerful thing to be able to use. For that reason, people in psychology do other kinds of experimentation as well. Still on the quantitative side, and experimentation is certainly quantitative, we can generate numbers some other different ways as well. In fact when I give that exercise I was just talking about in the last lecture about violence on television, I often have some folks who say, "Well now we did something very different. In fact, what we wanted to do was send out a log to the parents to say what kind of television shows you are watching." So this log might say, "Every half hour you have to write down what you watched in the previous half hour."

So at 10:30 you have to say what shows were on your television during that period of time.

Even today you could do it in a more automatic way by having some device on the television to tell you what has been watched during that period of time; some way you could collect data on what was being watched. Then you could take those data and compare it to some ratings you had for the amount of violence for each of those television shows and get some sort of a number saying that this is the mean rating for those television shows. For this particular family it was a 6.3 perhaps, and for another family it might be a 4.7 or something like that. Then what we are going to do is try to get some measure of the aggressiveness of the child. And so we are going to do some things like ask their teacher, "Give us a rating on how aggressive you think that child is on a 10-point scare." Or perhaps you could say how many trips to the principal's office the child has had or how many trips to juvenile center the child has had. Get some measure of aggressiveness of the child as well. Then what you can do is plot that on what is often called a "scatter plot." So on one axis you might have—say on the vertical axis—you might have how aggressive the child is, and on the horizontal axis you might have something like how violent the average television show that child watched. So for Jack you have 4.7 for how violent it was, and you go up and you have a 6.3 on how aggressive Jack is, and so you put a point there. Then for Susie, you come in here and maybe it is a 4.2 and 5.1, and you put a point there; and for Juan it is a 7.1. You get the idea.

So you end up with this graph, or the scatter plot, with points representing each data point is one of the children and how average violence was for that television show or for the television watching and how aggressive that child is. From that, you can try to determine whether there is a relationship between aggression and violence. In order to that we usually do a statistical test of some sort—and probably most of you are familiar with correlations—and what you figure out is a correlation coefficient, which is the result of this statistical test. We will not go into great detail; there are different correlation coefficients depending upon whether it is a linear relationship or a curvilinear relationship and so forth. For the most part you get a single number from this, and that the number goes from 0 to 1, and it is either positive or negative.

A correlation coefficient of 1 would indicate that there is a perfect relationship between these two. In fact, every data point would fall on a straight line for this particular correlation coefficient. Now, you would never get that in reality, but that is the ideal if you found a perfect relationship. The less perfect the relationship, it would go down to 0; 0 would indicate no relationship between the two variables. It would look like a shotgun pattern or something like that where there was no discernible trend line in these data points, and you would have either a positive or negative sign attached to this number. A positive sign would indicate that it was a relationship where one variable increased, the other variable increased as well. So the more violence on the television, the more aggression there was. A negative would indicate that the relationship was the opposite. If it is one increased the other one decreased. So that gives us some idea of the strength of the relationship and the direction of the relationship from the correlation coefficient.

However, I should point out that this is just a relationship. Suppose I ask you whether that meant—suppose we found a positive relationship. Suppose it was .73 or something like that, +.73—so we see that there is a relationship between the violent television shows and the amount of aggression. Does that mean that the violent television shows caused the aggressive behavior? I would hope that you would say, "No, it doesn't." You have not done an experiment here. This is called a "correlational observation." When you do a correlational observation, you have not manipulated an independent variable. I have not independently assigned anything in that thing I just described, that piece of research I just described. They decided what television shows to watch or their parents did. It was a behavior, not something I said at a particular level. They decided to do it. And aggressiveness, I did not set that, surely; that is a behavior as well. They behave that way; the teachers rated them and so forth. So they are both really dependent variables. We do not have an independent variable in the correlational observation. When you do not have an independent variable, you do not have an experiment. If you do not have an experiment, you cannot make a causal statement from that experiment. All you can say is that there are related, at least from a single piece of research like that. It can be multiple pieces of research; we'll talk about that in a minute and get some idea that perhaps its causal.

Now why is that? Why are the rules of science—we said that it was just a rule of science that you do an experiment, you can make a causal statement; but I just told you it was a rule of science that you cannot do that with a correlational observation—why not? Well, there are several problems with using a correlational observation and trying to infer causality. One of those problems is a directionality problem; you do not know which variable caused the other variable to change. It could be, in the case, let us say, of aggression and violence, maybe the more aggressive the kid is the more violent television shows they watch. So, in fact we have a real aggressive kid here. Johnny is an eight on aggression, and Johnny loves those shoot 'em up kinds of shows on television, so he watches the more aggressive shows. You have little Kenny down here who loves the nature shows on television and Sesame Street and that sort of thing and he hardly has any problems with aggression. So it is the amount of aggressiveness that is causing the violent television show, not the other way around. We have the directionality wrong.

That is one possible problem. A second problem can be a third variable that is entering into this. So it may be for example the aggressiveness of the parents that is causing both of this. Aggressive parents like watching violent television shows, and aggressive parents tend to treat their kids perhaps more punitively. So they punish their kids more; they spank their kids more. Maybe it is the aggressiveness of the parents that is causing both of these things, and that is the causality, not one of these causing the other one.

Now to illustrate that a little bit, let me tell you about a few cases where it is even clearer that there may be either directionality or a second variable kind of problem. One time the U.S. government, the military, was interested in what caused motorcycle accidents among the GIs; they were concerned with minimizing motorcycle accidents. So they went in and did a study, and it was a correlational observation. They sent out questionnaires, and they plugged in a lot of things: How old are you? What is your driving record like? Are you a man or a woman? And so forth. So they collect a lot of data to try to see what they could do in terms of predicting motorcycle accidents. Do you know what the number one predictor of motorcycle accidents was? It was how many tattoos the GI had. The more tattoos the GI had, the more motorcycle accidents the GI had. Now what are we to conclude from this? Are we to conclude that tattoos cause motorcycle accidents? Are we to conclude that motorcycle accidents cause tattoos? I do not think either of those is a very good hypothesis in this case. It is probably some third variable again. Perhaps, preference for bodily risk or something like that that is driving both of these. The more I am willing to risk my body and hang it out on the motorcycle, the more I am willing to risk it and have these tattoos that may cause their kind of problems. So these two things are related through a third variable.

If you look at a cigarette pack and the side of the cigarette pack is says very clearly now that smoking causes health problems, and it has various versions of that. I remember far enough back that there were no warning labels on cigarette packs, and I remember an intermediate stage where this is a warning that said smoking may cause health problems. Now how did we get from no warning to a causal statement that smoking causes health problems? The problem was of course that it was very difficult to do an experiment. You cannot tell a group of people—suppose you get a group of 500 people together and you say, "Alright, you are not allowed to smoke for the next 20 years." And another group of 500 you say, "You smoke one pack of cigarettes a day exactly for the next 20 years." And another group, "You smoke two packs of cigarettes a day for the next 20 years." That is an experiment. It is an independent variable. We manipulated it in this case at three levels. Nice experiment, but unfortunately, maybe fortunately, they will not let us do that. We are not allowed to dictate to people how much they can smoke. That is a personal choice. So we cannot do that experiment.

We can do some experiments perhaps with mice and force them to smoke and that sort of thing but there is always the problem of generalizing from an animal model to a human model, and so those data had to be looked at with some care. The only other data that were available were correlational observations. It was known for some time that there was a correlational observation that one thing was related to the other thing. So we knew many years ago that people who smoked more had more health problems, but you could not make the causal statement from a single correlational observation. There may be some third factor that is entering into this again. Maybe people who are more nervous tend to have more health problems. They are high-strung folks and they smoke more cigarettes. Maybe that is it. Maybe people who are less health conscious, they do not go to the doctor as much. They have more health problems because they do not seek personal care for their health, and perhaps they also smoke more because they are less concerned about their health.

So there may be some third factor that is driving both of these, and so that is again an illustration of where we got from a correlational observation to a causal statement. The only way they actually got there was to eliminate all of the other possible third factors through doing even more correlational observation. But it was a whole series of these that was required to even begin to make the causal statement, and even then there was a lot of flak from the cigarette companies when they wanted to make the causal statement even after looking at all of these correlational observations.

Surveys are usually done with correlational data. I am sure everybody has taken a survey. You may be asked to, from 1 to 7, say how much you agree with a particular statement on a survey, and those are certainly quantitative. We can add up those numbers, take means and that sort of thing, but in the end, all we have are correlational observations from surveys. We have not, again, manipulated any independent variable, and so we cannot do anything other than make correlational observations from those surveys. Surveys have some other kind of advantages and disadvantages as well. An advantage is you can actually ask people what they think about things. Suppose you are interested in, you are working in a grocery store and you want to know how to display your products nicely. So you do one sort of display and then another day you try a different kind of display, and now you may discover that the first display you sold more products from the second display. That would tell you something. It is kind of an experiment that you did there, but you do not know why, and so you might also pass out a survey and say: Did you think it looked better? Why did you buy this product? So you can sort of crawl into their heads a little bit more with a survey, but again, there are some problems, because all you get are their subjective opinions, and they certainly can lie to you about things. They may not know why they bought the product in fact. Or maybe buying the product was not particularly--it was a candy bar, and they were trying to be health conscious—and so they might lie to you about why they bought that particular product, for example.

So surveys have other kinds of problems as well but they certainly have a problem of being only a correlational observation. You could not make causal statements from it. Let me make one last comment about correlational observation before we move on to the other methodologies. People sometimes, if you read about these things in the newspaper, the article will get it right, but the headline will get it wrong because the headline writer read the article and inferred causality where there was no causality in the study being talked about. So you get a headline: Premarital Sex Causes Bad Grades in High School Children, or something like that. And you read the article and they discover they did a survey and they discovered that the kids who had premarital sex generally got lower grades, and they got a correlation on this basis, which is obviously a correlational observation. And then the headline writer wanted to spice it up a little bit and so jumped to the case of one caused the other. The use of smoking causes the use of hard drugs; all the kinds of headlines that you might see where, if you look at the study, it was not causal at all. So be wary when you see headlines that imply causality when you are talking about human behavior, because very often they may be talking about correlational observations.

Let us move on then to the qualitative techniques that are sometimes used in psychology. If I were giving this lecture 30 years ago, I would not be talking about qualitative methods at all in psychology. These are fairly recent, and their acceptance is still somewhat tenuous by psychologists. The more hardnosed experimenters in fact do not like qualitative data very much. But qualitative data are becoming more widely accepted in psychology so we ought to at least be aware of that.

Let me give you several kinds of qualitative data that can be produced, several different kinds of methodologies. There is a methodology called ethnography that attempts to observe and collect data from those within a particular culture or undergoing a common experience of some sort. I have a faculty member in my department who studies mother-daughter relationships, which is a fairly interesting kind of topic. It turns out that mothers and daughters do not get along too well at particular times in life. And so she brings people in, both mothers and daughters, brings them into the laboratory, and then she interviews them. She had some fairly structured questions that she asks them, and they can answer them in quite an open way. It is not like they are checking off an agree/disagree. It is not like it is just an oral version of a survey. In fact, these questions are asked, and then they may give a five-minute answer to the question. She tape-records this, and after they leave the laboratory, she transcribes this. And she has various ways that are too technical to get into today of analyzing the data from these kinds of exchanges. So she will analyze the data, put it into some different kinds of categories, for example, or do some actual analysis on the language used itself in order to better understand mother-daughter kinds of relationships. And that is ethnography at work even in the laboratory.

Ethnographers sometimes do things like set up focus groups, for example. Suppose I were a bank manager and I put in all of these ATM machines and I thought that was the greatest thing that came along and it was going to allow me to fire all of my tellers and save a whole lot of money and make things quite efficient for my bank. And then I discovered that we have all sorts of people who are not using the ATM machines. They still want to come in and talk to a teller, and we do not know why that is. Now you might do certain kinds of things to determine why that is. You might observe them trying to interact with the ATM machine or something like that; but one thing that you could do is set up a focus group. So you bring in some representative samples of people who use your bank and you ask them what the problem is here; why are you not using the ATM? Some may say, "Well, I did not feel safe using the ATM machine. It is not very well lit, there are not a lot of people around, I am afraid I am going to get robbed if I used the ATM machine." Others may say, "No, I really do not know how to use the ATM machine. I tried my best I could not get my money out of it. What is worse, I do not know how to put my money in it, I still do not know where my deposit goes when I put it in there. I get no receipt back, I do not like using that ATM machine for that reason." And you get other kinds of responses like that, which are fairly open-ended kinds of responses, but you can analyze them and perhaps categorize them to some extent, and it will give you some idea why they are using your ATM machine or not. So that is a focus group that is used.

Ethnographers can work in the laboratory or in the more natural setting; and when they start working in a more natural setting, in addition to calling it ethnography, we can call it "naturalistic observation." So they go to the particular place where the behavior is occurring and observe the behavior in a natural setting. And that has been done a number of different ways. For example, Jane Goodall— you are probably are familiar with her work with chimpanzees. Jane Goodall observed chimpanzees for many years, and an example of the kind of findings she might find in a naturalistic setting—she discovered that there was one particular chimpanzee she saw who would take a twig and pull off all of the leaves from the twig and stick this twig into a hole and the ants would crawl on the twig, and then it would lick all of the ants off and stick it back in the hole and lick the ants off and so forth. This was a first indication that animals other than humans used tools, and it was done in a naturalistic setting where she was unobtrusive observer in this setting, just watching the animals do this. Or you can, of course, do human behavior as well.

I attended a conference about a month ago where Napoleon Chagnon, who is a very famous anthropologist, had spent about 30 years studying the Yanomamo population in the Amazon. He just moved in with them, lived with them, observed them, took extensive notes about their behavior. And he, in the end, through ethnography, learned some very interesting things about this population. For example, people thought that if you study folks who do not have our modern day kind of civilization those folks would be fairly peaceful; sort of the "noble savage" model of what has been suggested by the philosophers, many centuries ago in fact, and which a lot of people liked to believe—Margaret Mead, who was a very famous anthropologist who claimed that the noble savage was out there. What Chagnon found, with this particular population, is that they were in fact very aggressive. There was a lot of killing that went on. The average male in this group, in fact, had participated in killing somebody else. So this very much knocked down this noble savage concept, and he did it through ethnography, through living with these people observing them.

Case history is another qualitative technique that is used as a methodology in psychology. Case histories are used for clinical cases. Freud—in fact we will talk about Freud in another lecture or two from now—extensively used case histories. His clinical case histories, in fact, formed the almost the entire basis of psychoanalytic theory, and it is one of the criticisms of psychoanalytic theory is that case histories are not very powerful research techniques. But sometimes they are the only things that we have. You could not set up an experiment to cause a mental illness and then investigate the mental illness—you have to take it as it comes to you—or any other kind of illness.

One of the earliest cases in psychology of interest is the case of Phineas Gage. Phineas Gage was a fellow who worked in the mining industry and was tamping in dynamite to blow up some rock, and the thing he was tamping with, which was a big, long rod, set off the dynamite and it blew this rod right up through Phineas's skull and right through his brain. And, amazingly enough, Phineas lived through this experience. People were amazed that this had happened and then they studied Phineas very extensively to find out what the problem was. He could still walk around; he could still talk. What they found is the particular area of his brain that it went through, he turned into a very different person; somebody who was quite irascible and quite aggressive and who was not the pleasant fellow he was before this. Well again, it's not ethical to cause somebody to have the kind of brain damage that Phineas Gage had, so you to had to kind of take it where it was. And in that case, case histories are fairly important methodologies in psychology.

Another thing that you can do is do critical incidents. These are case histories, not so much of a person, but it is a case history of something that happened. They do this very often with aircraft accidents when they are trying to investigate what happens. So they will go in and collect a bunch of near misses, where the accident did not quite happen, but it almost happened; and then they will bring these people in and do a critical incident analysis of it to find out what the conditions were as this incident was happening. That was often informative as well.

So these are all qualitative research techniques, and there are criticisms of these kinds of techniques. To begin with, none of them certainly are more than correlational observations at best. In many cases you do not even have the numbers that go along with correlational observations. So inferring causality is almost impossible with these kinds of studies. Secondly, if you do not really have numbers that you can rely on, how do you do statistical analyses on these kinds of data? So a lot of the modern statistical analyses that save psychologists, because they help to explain human variability, are not applicable to this kind of research. Finally, there is a lot of subjectivity to these kinds of things. The researchers' bias in sitting there doing ethnography can certainly influence the kinds of data that are being collected. And when it is a case history, there is also often a problem with memory, because you are talking about something that may have happened some time ago and the person has to remember; and memory, as we know, is somewhat suspect as well.

Now you do not have to rely on just one of these, you can do research that uses a number of different kinds, have a whole palette of different kinds of methodologies that can be used. Let me give you one quick example. There were people who are interested in motorcycle accidents and why people have motorcycle accidents under certain conditions; and motorcycles were being hit by cars, in particular. And so the question was, why is that and how do you collect data on such a thing? Well you can do case histories. I mean you can go find out from accident reports, you can get four or five different motorcycle accidents and then interview all of the participants and try to figure out why happened. It is kind of like a critical incident notion. Or you can go into the archives and look at all of the accident reports and try to figure out what the commonalities are for those accidents. Or you can even set up an experiment and have somebody come to a stop in a car, look both ways, judge the speed of the motorcycle as it is coming toward you, and find out whether they can judge the speed as you manipulate how fast that motorcycle is coming; in other words, an independent variable in that case. So you can use all of these kinds of techniques to try to find out why motorcycle accidents happen.

So we are not limited to one technique in psychology, we can use many. So, of these techniques, experimentation is very good; it is very precise and it allows us to infer causality. But it is somewhat artificial. Correlational observation can allow less artificiality, but we cannot infer causality. And some of the qualitative techniques can look at behavior in more naturalistic settings and under conditions that are more realistic, but we have various kinds of problems with those methodologies as well.

So those are the methodologies in psychology, and as we go through the rest of the course, you will be learning more about these methodologies as we talk about various research. Thank you.

Lecture Four
Evolutionary Theory and Modern Psychology

Scope:

During most of the history of psychology, human behavior has been considered to be largely a function of environmental influences, with few innate behaviors. Recently, there has been a trend to view behavior within an evolutionary context. Charles Darwin proposed the theory of evolution, which requires three simple factors: inheritability, genetic variation, and selection. Further improvements to the theory were made by Mendel, Lorenz, Hamilton, Trivers, and Wilson. Evolutionary psychologists believe that this approach can help explain why humans behave the way they do. One common misunderstanding is that evolutionary psychologists attribute behavior solely to genetics; in actuality, evolutionary psychologists believe that behavior results from the interplay of genes with the environment. Another misconception is that built-in behavioral dispositions cannot be changed. A third misconception is that built-in behaviors are optimal when, in fact, mismatches may occur as a result of rapidly changing environmental conditions. Evolutionary psychology is not without its critics: Some claim that it is just a theory; others say that it is too post hoc and, thereby, irrefutable; and others fear that it may be used to rationalize social injustices.

Outline

I. Because of the dominance of behaviorism and cognitive psychology through much of the history of psychology, the role of experience was given predominance over the role of built-in behavioral predispositions.

    A. Behaviorists took the Lockean position that the organism is a blank slate to be written upon by experience and concluded that the study of learning should be the cornerstone of psychology.

    B. Cognitive psychologists adopted as a metaphor the unprogrammed computer, in which experience writes the software programs, and the primary study of psychology is of the information processing done by these cognitive programs.

II. A recent trend in psychology is to view human behavior in an evolutionary context, in which behavior is the result of an interplay between built-in evolutionary adaptations and environmental constraints.

A. With his book *On the Origin of Species* (1859), Charles Darwin put forth the basic principles of evolution.

B. Darwin proposed that there are three basic processes required for evolution to take place.

  1. Although Darwin did not fully understand how it happens, he knew that there must be some way for inheritability to occur, for genetic material to be passed down through successive generations.

  2. There must be variation (through mutation or sexual reproduction) in the genetic process.

  3. There must be selection of some sort, such as natural selection.

C. Subsequently, a number of improvements and revisions have been made to Darwin's basic evolutionary theory that allow it to be more easily applied to human behavior.

D. An Austrian monk, Gregor Mendel, discovered that inheritance was *particulate*, that is, carried by discrete units called *genes* that are passed down to subsequent generations in an all-or-none manner.

E. An ethologist, Konrad Lorenz, discovered that many animals have innate behavior patterns that have developed as evolutionary adaptations and are triggered by environmental cues.

  1. One of Lorenz's more famous studies involved goslings following the first moving object they saw after hatching, which happened to be Lorenz, a phenomenon called *imprinting*.

  2. In this case, a fixed behavior pattern (the following behavior), occurred in the presence of a sign stimulus (Lorenz).

F. In 1964, the biologist William D. Hamilton proposed *inclusive fitness theory*, asserting that fitness includes not only an individual's reproductive success but also the reproductive success of genetic relatives, which introduced gene-level thinking.

G. In the early 1970s, Robert Trivers proposed three theories that extended evolutionary thinking: reciprocal altruism, parental investment theory, and parent-offspring conflict.

   1. *Reciprocal altruism theory* claims that reciprocal altruism has an adaptive advantage: If you do something good for someone, he or she will do something good for you later.

   2. *Parental investment theory* claims that because women invest more time than men in the reproductive process and the raising of offspring, men and women may have differing value systems in picking mates.

   3. The *parent/offspring conflict theory* suggests that conflicts arise because parents are related equally to all their offspring, while the offspring are related to each other by only 50% but to themselves by 100%; thus, their values are not equal to those of their parents.

H. In 1975, Edward O. Wilson published *Sociobiology: The New Synthesis*, proposing that evolutionary concepts could be applied to all animals, including humans.

I. Evolutionary thinking offers psychology the possibility of explaining not only the *what* and *how* of human behavior but also the *why*.

III. Several common misunderstandings have arisen about evolutionary theory as applied to human behavior.

   A. One misunderstanding is a false nature-versus-nurture dichotomy.

      1. Human behavior requires both evolved adaptations that are built into the individual and environmental conditions that activate these adaptations.

      2. Sun-tanning is an example of the interaction of an adaptation, melanin synthesis, with the environment, causing uv_b exposure.

3. In a similar way, it is naïve to ask whether intelligence is the result of nature or nurture.

B. A second misunderstanding is that if an adaptation is built in, we cannot change it.

   1. Because all behavior results from an interplay of nature with nurture, we can change behavior.

   2. In the case of sun-tanning, we can control the shade of our skin by staying inside, covering our bodies, using sunscreen, and so on.

   3. We can also change intelligence by manipulating the environment.

C. A third misunderstanding is that current adaptations are optimal.

   1. Evolutionary change is a slow process, but the environment can change rapidly; for this reason, we can point to many cases of mismatches between adaptations that were optimal during a previous adaptation period and the current environment.

   2. An example of a mismatch is humans' craving for fat and sugar and the minimization of unnecessary exercise, which was appropriate for an environment in which food was scarce, and the current environment, in which fat and sugar and exercise-saving machines are readily available, with the result obesity.

IV. We will discuss evolutionary psychology in more detail in future lectures, but in the meantime, keep in mind these caveats:

A. Although evolutionary theory is the most widely accepted theory in the scientific belief system about how we got to be the way we are, the scientific belief system itself is just a belief system and may compete with other personal belief systems.

B. Evolutionary psychology is sometimes criticized as being too post hoc and, because of this, able to explain any type of behavior.

C. There is a danger of applying the naturalistic fallacy that justifies our nature: If it is built in, it must be okay.

Essential Reading:

David M. Buss, *Evolutionary Psychology: The New Science of the Mind*.

Supplementary Reading:

Charles Darwin, *On the Origin of Species*.

Steven J. C. Gaulin and Donald H. McBurney, *Psychology: An Evolutionary Approach*.

John Dupré, *Human Nature and the Limits of Science*.

Questions to Consider:

1. What evidence would it take to convince you that a particular behavior (for example, monogamy) is an evolutionary adaptation rather than environmentally learned?

2. For what behaviors besides eating is there a mismatch between today's environment and our ancestors' environment of evolutionary adaptation?

Lecture Four—Transcript
Evolutionary Theory and Modern Psychology

In today's lecture, we are going to talk about the influences of evolutionary theory on psychology, and in particular on modern psychology. Now, that may seem to be kind of strange, because evolutionary theory was proposed back in the mid-1800s by Charles Darwin. How is it that it is having its influences on psychology only now? Well actually, it did have influences on early psychology and a particular psychoanalytic that we are going to talk about later in the course.

Psychoanalytic theory alludes to instinctive kinds of things; much as the id, when we talk about psychoanalytic theory, is instinctive in nature. So there was some influence of Darwin and evolutionary theory on psychology in early psychology. However, the behaviorists then came along in about 1910 or so, and they so took over psychology that we ignored altogether anything being built in, because they very much assumed the John Locke position of having a *tabula rasa*, or a blank slate, and this was to be written upon by learning. So learning became the cornerstone of psychology, and for almost half a century only learning was studied in psychology, and people forgot all about evolutionary theory. There are reasons for this, not only in psychology, but there are some political reasons for that as well that we will not go into today.

Then, in the 1960s, you will recall that cognitive psychology came along, and cognitive psychology also operated to some extent on a blank slate principle. Again, we have talked about this a little bit in the past, and the computer metaphor being used in cognitive psychology where you had the large mainframe computer, but not much was built-in. And, in fact, this was written upon by human experience in terms of an analog of forming software programs with your human experience. So people did not think much about evolutionary psychology, and evolutionary theory had little to do with psychology. This has changed, and in the 1990s in particular the theory of evolutionary psychology actually was named, and there has been a great deal of research in evolutionary psychology today.

Now I want to talk about evolutionary psychology a little bit at this point, in order to prepare you for looking at some of the more traditional areas of psychology, because I think it is informative to do that, and look at some of these from an evolutionary sense. So we are going to go over some of the basics of the theory today, what Darwin actually said was required for evolution. Then we are going to look some at some of the people who have adapted evolutionary theory in recent times to the human and human behavior. Then we are going to look at several misunderstandings about evolutionary theory as applied to human behavior, and why those misunderstandings are indeed misunderstandings. And finally we will discuss evolutionary psychology in terms of the way belief systems are changed and some terms are like naturalistic fallacy. So, let me get started by talking some about what Darwin actually said.

In 1859 Charles Darwin published his book called the *On the Origin of Species*. Charles Darwin was a naturalist, and he had studied in school in order to be able to look at plants and animals and how they develop the way they do. And he took a cruise on a boat called the *Beagle,* and went to, in particular, the Galapagos Islands. And while on the Galapagos Islands, he studied all sorts of different natural phenomena and collected lots of different kinds of species and did extensive writing. And when he came back, he had to try to decide what this all meant. What he eventually came up with was the theory of evolution. Now there is somebody else who came along about the same time and proposed the theory of evolution, but Charles Darwin is usually given the credit for being the father of evolution.

He proposed that there were really just three basic processes required for evolution. It is really pretty simple but widely misunderstood by people. The first of those processes is inheritability; you have to have some way that the genetic message is passed down from parent to offspring. Charles Darwin, rather surprisingly, did not know much about how this happened, and he was mistaken about how this happened. We will see in just a minute, when I talk about Mendel, that this was an update really on Charles Darwin. They lived about the same time, but in fact he was not familiar, at least did not use Mendel's work in his theory of evolution. But he knew that somehow the message had to be transmitted from the parent to the offspring.

A second thing that is required is variation. This variation occurs through mutation or through sexual reproduction, and in this way variation is passed down to the offspring. In terms of mutation, what happens is a mistake is made, basically. When the genetic material is selected from one of the parents or the other, a change is made in the genetic material and a different adaptation is made which might cause a structural or behavioral difference in the offspring, which is simply a matter of a mistake. You also get some variation by sexual reproduction. One of the nicer things about sexual reproduction, other than the obvious, is the fact that it produces variation. You have the parents each making a contribution to the genetic outcome of the offspring, and there is sort of a roulette wheel that is spun every time we have a child, and it picks off genetic messages from the parents and from the grandparents, and we get kind of a hodgepodge of genetic messages that do produce some variation.

So inheritability, variation; and the third thing that is required is some form of selection. Now, this selection, in Darwin's sense, is naturalistic selection; natural selection, or what is sometimes called "survival of the fittest." But it does not have to be that. You could have selection that is not natural. You can have breeding for example. For example, we take racehorses; and we try to breed racehorses, and we breed them so they have these little, thin legs and very powerful muscles and are very fast, and they are good for racing unless they break their leg. They are not very good for plow horses. We breed them for a specific purpose, and this is a form of selection. Usually you have natural selection, and all this means is that once one of these mistakes is made, and you get variation, that mistake will stick around if it allows the offspring to be more successful. They survive longer and reproduce better than it is selected through natural selection, and stays as part of evolution.

So those are the basic three things that are required for evolution, and only those three things. Now subsequently, that was a long time ago that Darwin suggested these things, and since then there have been a number of things that have happened that kind of update evolution, and in particular update evolution so that it can include humans. The first one happened about the same time as Darwin, and that is Gregor Mendel, who was an Austrian monk who was studying inheritance. And he used plants for the most part to do this, and I am sure you are all somewhat familiar with what Mendel did. He bred plants that were tall and plants that were short and came up with a notion that the genetic material was particulate; that is you do not get mixed messages, you get one message depending upon what genetic material has been selected for the offspring. Up until that time, and Darwin thought that this was the case, a lot of people thought that there was blending. That you had a father and a mother, and the offspring were some blended combination. So if you have a very tall mother and a very short father, as they are genes are blended, you would get a medium sized offspring; and that is not true. As Mendel showed, they get either the tall gene or the short gene, at least if it is a single gene case—and polygenic traits there are various genes that may be combined in different ways—but for the simple cases, you only get one gene and it is a particulate. It is either the mother's gene or the father's gene. And that was somewhat new to people, and we now understand more about the inheritability part of evolutionary theory because of Gregor Mendel's work.

Ethologist Konrad Lorenz, far more recently—he is an ethologist and he was studying animal behavior for the most part—he was one of the first to show that there are innate behavior patterns that have developed as evolutionary adaptations, and that these are triggered by environmental cues. One of his more famous studies—he took goslings that had just been born to the mother goose, and as they are hatched, the goslings look around, and one of the things that is built into them is an innate tendency to follow the first large moving object that crosses their field, and that happened to be Conrad Lorenz in fact. So, as Conrad Lorenz walked around, these goslings all lined up behind him and followed him along. You may have seen the picture of him walking along with a whole string of goslings following him along. They had this built into them, a fixed behavior pattern that simply says, "follow the large moving object as soon as you are born." It is called "imprinting." And so they do this, and it does not matter to them whether it is the mom or Conrad Lorenz, they are the equivalent to this fixed action pattern that simply follows this, what is called sign stimulus. And this was one of the first times; and Lorenz showed this not only in goslings, but also in lots of other animals, that there are these fixed behavior patterns that can occur at least in animals.

Biologist William Hamilton in the mid-'60s proposed a kind of a new twist to evolutionary theory, and that is a topic called inclusive fitness. Up until this time, it was thought that fitness was pretty much parent to child; so if you had an adaptation that was passed down to your offspring that would increase that child's fitness, that then was direct fitness. But what Hamilton showed was that there is also a topic of inclusive fitness. Inclusive fitness says that it is important, not only the reproductive success of your direct offspring, but also the reproductive success of genetic relatives. For example if you are going to be altruistic, you might be altruistic and do good things for your children because indeed they are genes that are being carried along, but you might also do good things for your brother or your sister who share a part of your genes; and you might do good things for your sister or brother's offspring as well, your nieces and nephews, because they share some of your genes. So this altruistic behavior should be spread around. This got people to thinking about the genes in a somewhat different way, and it sort of became the new unit of evolution. Up until this time, the individual was kind of the unit of evolution; that, in fact, it was the survival of the individual that was important. This adaptation to this theory said it is the genes' survival that is important. The gene is the basic genetic unit, and we are just big bags of water. We are life support systems to carry around genes for a finite period of time; we are mortal after all. The genes are seeking to be immortal, and so they are far more concerned about your reproduction and the next generation that they can live in and become immortal. So the unit of survival is now the gene, not the individual, and that makes a big difference in terms of the way you look at evolution.

Robert Trivers came along in the 1970s and proposed three theories that also extended evolutionary thinking. One of these was reciprocal altruism. I just mentioned altruism with respect to your own kin. Reciprocal altruism has to do whether we can do good things for other people, and he said that there was an adaptive advantage to reciprocal altruism; that if you do something good for somebody else, they were likely to do something good for you. In evolutionary times, suppose you come back from the hunt with a big leg of meat, and you bring that back and you do not have any storage facilities. You cannot eat the whole leg, your own family, and so you might invite other people to share this leg of meat with you, and you do not get any direct benefit at the time. Why should you do that? Well, because next week, maybe this individual will come back from the hunt with his own leg of meat and might share with you. So reciprocal altruism became important.

Also, parental investment theory was suggested. With parental investment theory, this says that woman and men invest far differently in their offspring. Women invest at least nine months, and with lactation, probably more like at least three or four years in raising the offspring; and actually, in fact, probably more like 10 years in raising an offspring. And men, on the other hand, at least in terms of minimal investment, may invest 30 seconds or a minute in producing offspring. And if that is the case, we would expect different patterns of behavior for women and for men. We might expect pickier women in terms of picking men who will provide resources for the offspring during this period of time that she is investing in them. The man might have different values if this is the case. He might find it more important to have women who are attractive and who, in fact, are quite fertile. That might be a different value system that would be suggested by parental investment theory.

Finally, he also suggested parent-offspring conflicts. This is obvious because in fact the parent is related to each of their offspring by the same amount. So as a parent, I think my two sons ought to share equally in things. They do not think that. My son, because he is related 100% to himself, my older son thinks he ought to get twice of everything that his younger brother gets because he is only related 50% to his younger brother. And the younger brother feels the same way about the older brother. So we get into conflicts, because I think they ought to share, and they think they ought to distribute the resources in a different way.

In 1975, E.O. Wilson published *Social Biology: The New Synthesis*, and this was a quite controversial book at the time, because he included a chapter in evolution with respect to humans. This was one of the first times that it was suggested that evolution could be applied to humans. It is really the beginning—even though he is a biologist, he is not a psychologist—but it was the beginning of evolutionary psychology. Evolutionary thinking, as I have mentioned before in a former lecture, is a way of asking "why" questions, as well as "what" and "how" questions, and that is part of the reason it is kind of exciting.

Let me now talk about some of the misunderstandings about evolutionary theory as applied to human behavior. One common misunderstanding is a false nature/nurture dichotomy, and people often get it wrong with respect to evolutionary theory. They think that people who are supporting evolutionary theory think that if it is built-in, the environment has nothing to do with it, when in fact most modern day evolutionary theorists thinks it is both nature and the nurture. The old nature versus nurture arguments have really gone by the wayside as quite naïve. But it is always nature and nurture according to modern day evolutionary theorists. A good example of this is sun tanning. If I asked you, "Is it nature or nurture that gives you the color of your skin," you might say "Well, I suppose it is nature." But, in fact, if you stay out in the sun longer, you turn darker, at least light-skinned people do. They do that because of an adaptation. We have, built in to us, melanin synthesis, so that when we are exposed to uv_b sunlight, our skin turns darker. That happens because it helps us to avoid skin cancer. The darker we turn the less of the uv_b that we get, and it is uv_b that causes skin cancer. So this is nature's way of giving us an umbrella to protect us from the sun and keep us from getting skin cancer. So why are we not all just dark as can be? Well because there is another thing that the sun does for us as well, and that is Vitamin D; and we get vitamin D from the sun, and that is an important nutrient that we need to survive. So we have to get some sunlight, but not too much sunlight. And so there is an adaptation built into us through melanin that allows us to put more of the sun's shade up or less of the sun's shade up by changing the color of our skin.

Now if I asked, "Is the color of your skin due to built in kinds of things to nature?" Sure is. If you did not have this adaptation you would not turn darker. Is it due to the environment? Oh, of course it is due to the environment. If you did not have the sun turning your skin darker, it would not get in darker. So, in fact, it is nature and nurture, not nature versus nurture. And we can point that out in nearly every case that adaptations are not adaptations, where they set off some pattern that is irrevocable, but in fact that pattern; that adaptation works with the environment, and it is the combination of those two things that causes our behavior.

In a similar way, intelligence is certainly not all built in. People get very upset about these kinds of arguments sometimes, and we are trying to indicate that intelligence is due to the intelligence of your parents. Well, it is due to that, but it is also due to the environment that you grow up in. That is why we do things like hang mobiles over children's cribs and things like that—to try to change their intelligence through the environment. So it is a combination of those things.

The second misunderstanding is that if an adaptation is built in, then you cannot change it, that if it is that way, then you cannot step in and do something else. And again, that is not true; we do have the ability to use logical thought to override behavioral adaptations. These behavioral adaptations give us predispositions to behave in a particular way, but are not deterministic in saying you have to behave that way. This is quite apparent when you have the ability to change things like the intelligence through the environment.

A third misunderstanding is that current adaptations, the way you are now, is optimal. And that is certainly not the case. Why? Because the current adaptations are due to our ancestral history, not due to today's environment. If you put the whole year, if you take a year and claim that it is the time that humans have been around—which is about 5 million years, some form of human has been around—and you put that on a year, and you ask where certain kinds of modern things that have happened in that year's time. For example, when did agriculture occur during the year period of time? Agriculture occurred as I recall about 9:00 on the last day of the year. Prior to that there was no agriculture. You did not till the fields prior to that. When did cities and civilization occur? That occurred at about 11:30, as I recall, during this year. When did the Industrial Revolution occur? That occurred within minutes of midnight during this year. Where did our adaptations occur? They occurred through most of this year's period of time; not during the last half-day of this period of time. So it is not surprising that we have mismatches of the way we behave in the way today's society is. It is not optimal the way we behave.

Let me give you an example of that. We love fat and sugar in our diets. I mean, I eat. I would love to be able to eat—I do not do it because I override it; it can be changed—but I would love to eat every piece of bacon I see. I would love to be able to eat every Twinkie I see. I love, and you do too, fat and sugar, and we are built that way on purpose. Our ancestors seldom ran across fat and sugar. The animals, even meats, back in those days had 5% or less fat. Not the 40% fat that we get in our well-bred meat today. They did not get sugar. We eat about two-thirds of a cup of sugar every week. They did not have refined sugar; they would run across a beehive every now and then, or have a little sugar with their food. But they did not have sugar readily available in their diets. So every time they had a chance at it, they ate it.

They also had an adaptation that said do not move if you do not have to. They were the ultimate couch potatoes, because that is the way you survive. When you have to go out and hunt, you go out and hunt. But when you do not, you lie around and do not waste that energy. So we have that built into to use too. And if you look at today's society that causes all sorts of problems; in particular, obesity and other health problems. Why, we are having current wave of—we get better and better at putting more sugar and fat into our diet—we get better and better at not having to move a bit once we sit down. And as we do that, we have all sorts of health problems that are caused. Is that optimal? It most certainly is not optimal. And so in fact, that is a mismatch. And we will point out other mismatches as well as we get into more detail about evolution later.

Let us talk about just a few things having to do with some caveats that we want to make with respect to evolutionary theory. For one thing, evolutionary theory, we have to agree, is in fact the most widely accepted theory about how we got to be the way we are. However, the scientific belief system itself is just a theory, and there are other belief systems that we might hold. If you are going to be an educated person you probably better know about evolutionary theory as one of the major components of scientific to scientific belief systems. But if you will recall back when we were talking about experimentation, for example, we said that if you manipulate an independent variable, measure a dependent variable, then you can say that it was the independent variable that caused the dependent variable. Why did we agree that we could do that? Well because that is what we believe. Basically scientists got together and said that we are going to believe this thing; it seems to work, and so we are going to decree that that is the way it is and that is our belief system. That is the scientific belief system. But there are other personal belief systems that people can have, and that might compete and perhaps run in parallel with the scientific belief system that people can have; and that might compete and perhaps run in parallel with the scientific belief system.

Evolutionary psychology is also sometimes criticized as being too *post-hoc*, "after the fact." But, in fact, my grandmother could have told me those kinds of things. So, we already know an awful lot about human behavior; and so we kind of know how humans are going to behave to begin with. And we go back to evolutionary theory, and we say what can we justify from evolutionary theory to explain this kind of behavior. And we discover that we can explain it quite nicely. The problem is that if we had behaved differently in the first place, and we knew that we were, we might have gotten a different cover story from evolutionary psychology, and that people who are critical of this say that because it is so post-hoc we can explain anything we might want to explain. And that probably was a criticism fairly early on in evolutionary psychology. However, that is advanced to the point now where lots of behaviors that are not obvious are being explained, and I think that is a weakening kind of criticism of evolutionary theory.

Finally, there is a danger in applying what is called the "naturalistic fallacy." The naturalistic fallacy says basically that, if it is natural, that must be the way it is supposed to be. And so, we justify things that we should not be justifying using the naturalistic fallacy. Now we have already talked a little bit about why that is not an appropriate way to do things, because of things like mismatches. So if we have different behaviors, say, for men and women, that are predicted by adaptations that have occurred, left over from ancestral times, it is inappropriate for us to say, "Well that is the way it should be. It is okay for women to be that way, it is okay for men to be that way, because that is what built in," because there may be an entire mismatch with the way we want our society to be or the way modern day societies are. Just like it is not okay to eat all of the fat and all of the sugar that is provided; there is a mismatch. It is not the society we want to have today, unless we want to have everybody lying in bed highly obese. So in fact the naturalistic fallacy is a fallacy.

What I think is most important is understanding what the causes of behaviors are, at least behavior predispositions. If you want to change society, it's best to know what our behavioral adaptations are to begin with if we want a society that is different from that. To go in naively and pretend that there are no built in adaptations probably hurts us in trying to build the kind of society we want to build.

So, what we have done today is go quickly over evolutionary theory, we have done this so that we might be able to apply some of this as we are talking about the rest of psychology. We talked a little bit about how the behaviorists and the cognitive psychologists kind of accepted a *tabula rasa*, a blank slate, and how Charles Darwin came along and suggested that there might be some things built in; how those built-in things are accomplished through inheritability, variation, and selection. And then we talked about some of the more modern adaptations that have changed the basic theory of evolution. And we talked about some of the misunderstandings that occur with evolutionary thinking, including the false nature/nurture dichotomy, how some people think you cannot change it and how some people think that it is optimal.

And finally, we talked about some caveats you have to employ when you talk about evolutionary thinking. So, we are going to leave it at there, and I hope you will consider these things as we go onto the other topics in this course. Thank you.

Lecture Five
Freud's Thinking

Scope:

Historically, the most prominent theory of personality is psychoanalytic theory, proposed by Sigmund Freud around 1900. Freud was a medical doctor who had patients with hysteria and, partly as a result of studying hypnotism, he began to believe that the unconscious level drives most of human behavior. Although Freud may not have been the first to propose the unconscious, he was the one who emphasized it as the largest component of the personality. This notion is now a major underlying concept that has led to many current policies and institutions. Freud also proposed that our personalities are made up of three parts. The *id* acts on a pleasure principle and, if unchecked, would cause us to behave in a hedonistic way. The *superego* operates on a moral principle and uses guilt to enforce rule-bound behavior. The *ego* operates on a reality principle and mediates between the id and the superego to determine appropriate behavior.

Outline

I. One of the major areas of psychology is the study of theories of personality, of which there are many.

    A. For good or ill, the name most associated with psychology is Sigmund Freud, the father of the most famous personality theory, *psychoanalytic theory*, and psychoanalysis.

        1. Freud was born in Moravia in 1856; moved to Vienna, Austria, at the age of four when his father's business failed; and studied medicine at the University of Vienna.

        2. Freud was a rather unsuccessful physician in private practice until he began working with women having hysteria.

        3. He studied hypnotism in Paris with Charcot, which helped to convince him of the power of the unconscious.

        4. In 1900, he published *The Interpretation of Dreams* and, in 1901, *The Psychopathology of Everyday Life*, both of which introduced psychoanalytic theory.

B. The major cornerstone of psychoanalytic theory is the notion that our behavior is driven mainly by sexual and aggressive energy manifested at the unconscious level of the mind.

    1. The unconscious is sometimes characterized as the submerged part of an iceberg; the part above water is the conscious level; and the waterline is a censoring mechanism preventing thoughts in the unconscious from entering the conscious level.

    2. Freud believed that at the unconscious level, there are instincts from birth, one of which is the life force, or *libido*. This is largely made up of sexual energy.

    3. Freud also talked about the death instinct, which exists at the unconscious level and may cause suicide or lead to aggressive behavior. Freud believed that efforts to suppress this instinct lead to conflict.

    4. Although Freud is credited with inventing the notion of the unconscious, he was not the first to discuss the importance of the unconscious, as noted in an 1870 book by Henry Maudsley, *Body and Mind*.

    5. Freud believed that all of behavior is determined, that there are no mistakes or accidents.

    6. The notion of the unconscious permeates our society and forms the underpinnings of many of our institutions, such as our judicial system, prisons, and mental institutions.

II. Beyond the concept of the unconscious, Freud proposed that our personalities were made up of three conflicting entities.

    A. The earliest and most basic part of the personality is the *id*.

        1. The id operates on a pleasure principle: If it feels good, do it.

        2. The id is built in at birth and is part of our basic physiology.

        3. If we were solely id, we would take whatever we wanted in life without any consideration of others.

    B. During childhood, with proper instruction from our parents and society, the *superego* is formed.

1. The superego operates on a moral principle and is a concept essentially equivalent to the conscience.

2. The superego contains all the rules, the dos and don'ts taught to us early in our lives.

3. The superego has guilt as its weapon against the pleasures of the id.

4. Obviously, the id and the superego have major conflicts, because many of the ways the id wants to behave are against the rules of the superego.

C. Acting as a mediator between the id and the superego is the *ego*.

1. The ego operates on a reality principle.

2. One role of the ego is to act as the referee between the id and the superego, giving each enough control to allow the game of life to be played.

3. As the ego develops strength, it begins to carry around a self-concept that can be used as a standard, so that each conflict between the id and superego does not have to be individually mediated.

Essential Reading:

Sigmund Freud, *Introductory Lectures on Psychoanalysis*.

Supplementary Reading:

F. C. Crews, *Unauthorized Freud*.

Robert Nye, *Three Psychologies: Perspectives from Freud, Skinner, and Rogers*, 4th ed., chapter 3.

Questions to Consider:

1. Do you think that most of behavior is driven by an unconscious level, and if so, what evidence would you cite to support that belief?

2. If hypnotism and dreams are not products of the unconscious, how else would you explain them?

Lecture Five—Transcript
Freud's Thinking

At this point in the course we have covered some of the history of psychology and looked at some of the precursors in philosophy and some of the history of both experimental and clinical psychology. We've looked at some of the methodologies that are used in psychology, both the quantitative methodologies of experimentation and correlational observation, and some of the qualitative methodologies that are used as well.

Then we had a lecture on evolutionary theory and how that might impact our thinking about human behavior. Today, we want to look at another conception of who we are, and this is a very old one in psychology. This is Sigmund Freud's Psychoanalytic Theory, and psychoanalytic theory has had a major impact on psychology. Today, psychoanalytic theory is not used nearly as much as it originally was, and in fact even the therapy based upon psychoanalytic theory, psychoanalysis, is not in as much use as it was originally in psychology. And some of my colleagues in fact are surprised that I am still lecturing on psychoanalytic theory, but I think it is an important theory to think about. After all, if you ask the average person name one psychologist they will name Sigmund Freud. That is the one that immediately comes to mind even more so that Joyce Brothers and Dr. Phil. Sigmund Freud is somebody that they remember, and when I tell people I am a psychologist, they will immediately jump to the conclusion that I am a clinical psychologist and I am somehow intimately linked with Sigmund Freud, even though it could be my training as far distant from psychoanalytic theory.

I think psychoanalytic theory, over and beyond that, is also important because it has affected many of our social institutions. And in fact, some of the basic tenets of psychoanalytic theory are tenets we still believe in, in many of our social institutions. In fact, when I start to talk about psychoanalytic theory in my classes, I often come in and I say, "Alright. I have decided to run for governor and I have a new plan and we are going to save a lot of money and move money from the prisons over to education. And the way that we are going to do that—it is a very simple plan—I have decided that we ought to beat our prisoners whenever they misbehave and the punishment will cause them to behave properly. Nobody likes to get beat, so this sounds like a good idea to me. So that is my new plan; we are going to beat the prisoners until they behave properly, and then we will allow them to go back out in society and empty out our prisons." I say, "What do you think of that plan?"

And they, of course, immediately jump to the ethical considerations and said, "You cannot do that, that is inhumane." I'll say, "Well ignore that for a minute. Let us just talk about whether or not that would work. Do you think it would work?" They say, "Well no, I really do not think so."

I say, "Well why? If you were beat, wouldn't you decide to behave properly so you could stop being beaten?" They say, "Well it sounds right, but I do not think so, I do not think it would work." "Well why wouldn't it work?" "Well, I do not know, people just do not think that way." "Well how do they think? What is causing their behavior if that is not the case?" "Well there is something that is kind of beyond their control that is causing their behavior." "Well what is that?"

And sometimes they even come up with the word, "Well there is something at the unconscious level that is doing this." And they have immediately jumped to Freudian concept here. That is his key concept in fact in psychoanalytic theory, is that our behavior is driven at the unconscious level. The unconscious level is one of the most important drivers of our behavior, and if you want to correct behavior, you have to do it at the unconscious level. You cannot do it at the conscious, rational level and get people to make rational decisions, because part of this is out of their control. That is a very Freudian concept, as we will see. So I think psychoanalytic theory has been very important for our social institutions, our penal systems, our mental institutions, and so forth; and we make a lot of assumptions about this and when we are trying to correct people's behavior.

So let us go back and talk a little bit then about Freud and his life. We are going to talk some about that; then we will talk more about the unconscious level. And finally we will talk about the three components of our personality. This is a personality theory after all, and there are a number of personality theories. But this is one the ones that is most cited in psychology.

Sigmund Freud was born in Moravia, which is now Czechoslovakia, back in 1856. He was born to a Jewish family. His father was a wool merchant and was not very successful. In fact, when he was four years old, his father lost his job and they had to move to Vienna to try to get another job, and they were not in real good circumstances either. This was his father's second marriage, he had two boys by his first marriage; and by his second marriage, there were eight kids from that marriage. So they had 10 kids in this family.

But Freud, to his credit, Sigmund Freud went on and got a good education and then tried to decide what to become. As a Jewish boy, he did not have much choice. If he wanted to be a professional in those days about the only option was to become a doctor. So that is what he decided to do. He went to medical school and got a medical degree and became a medical doctor. His particular specialty was neurology. He was studying the nervous system, originally sort of the organic basis of things, like neurosis and other neurological disorders. But he became increasingly interested in non-organic and the psychological roots of neurosis and other nervous system disorders. And he was dealing with a set of usually middle class, upper middle class women in his practice, and discovering that many of them had what was classified as "hysteria."

This is a kind of old classification. We will mention this again when we talk about classification systems in a later lecture, but it is now called "conversion disorder," and it was considered to be a disease solely of women—that is why it is named hysteria, after *hystera*, which is the uterus. And so it is expected that women had this, but men did not have it; and a conversion disorder, or hysteria, some part of the body quits working. It is considered to be a conversion because it has converted a psychological problem into a physical problem. This may cause blindness or the inability to hear, or perhaps a left arm is paralyzed or something like that and they cannot find any organic neurological reason for this, but it apparently has a psychological cause to it. So those are the kinds of problems he was interested in and trying to solve those using psychology.

Very early in his practice, he discovered that there was a fellow named Charcot—Jean Charcot—who was practicing in Paris and using hypnosis in his practice. And so Freud went for a year to study with Charcot in Paris, and he found Charcot giving all sorts of demonstrations. Let me give you an example. Charcot was in a room and he had an audience, and he brought a woman down and put her into a hypnotic trance, and then told her that when the clock struck one, she would get up and open the window. And he took her out of trance, had her sit down there, and sure enough, when the clock struck one, she went over and opened up the window and sat back down again. Then Charcot said now why did you open the window? And she said, "Well I thought it was kind of hot and stuffy in here and I thought we needed some air and that is the reason."

Freud was impressed; number one, that he got her to open the window, and number two, that she had no recollection of why she had opened the window, but in fact she rationalized why she opened the window. She had already behaved in particular way, so she used her rational mind to try to come up with a reason for her behavior. He also discovered that Charcot could simulate conversion disorder or hysteria in people who did not have it by putting them under hypnosis, and he could get somebody, for example, under the hypnotic state to have their left arm become useless while they were in the hypnotic state. So again, he thought that there might be psychological origins at the unconscious level for this kind of disorder. This was an important breakthrough for him.

So he went back and opened up a private practice. He practiced with a fellow named Breuer for a while, and they both were using hypnosis in their practice to try to get at this hysteria problem; and that seemed to work okay. He would put somebody into a hypnotic state and then have them try to talk through his or her problems. But there were difficulties with that as well. He did not think that people really confronted their problems as well in the hypnotic state. So, in fact, he moved on to other methods, and thought that maybe it was the talking part of the thing that was helping solve their problems more than being in a hypnotic state. So he eventually did away with hypnosis altogether and just started talking therapy, which is psychoanalysis, as we know it today, where there are things like "free association" that we will talk about a little bit more later.

So that is what sort of the early career of Freud. And if we look at the unconscious a little more clearly, let us envision what this might look like. One way the people do this is to imagine an iceberg; so we have this big mass of ice that is sitting in the water, and below the waterline is about 90% of this iceberg and above the waterline is about 10% of the iceberg. The way this is used is the part below the waterline is generally conceptualized as the unconscious, and the part of above the waterline, that 10%, is the conscious level. The waterline represents a censoring mechanism that keeps us from figuring out what is going on at the unconscious level; prevents you from getting the unconscious level.

Now there are other variations of this. There is the pre-conscious, which sometimes comes into play. That is a level where you can get to the preconscious level if you work hard enough, but it is something that is not currently in your conscious level. But we will keep it fairly simple, and just pretty much talk about the unconscious level. The unconscious level, as we have talked about, is what primarily drives our behavior, and we do not have direct access to it. And so there is a problem if you want to correct behavior, if you want to change behavior, if the primary driver of behavior is what is happening at the unconscious level and you do not have direct access to it. How do you get to it to do something about it? That is a conundrum that Freud had to figure out how to do that, and that is where he came up with psychoanalytic theory.

At the unconscious level, we have things seething down there, and these are due to various kinds of energy that we have. These are instinctual kinds of things. So Freud was not a blank slate theorist at all. He thought that there were, in fact, instincts that were there from birth. One of these instincts is a life force, or a life instinct, that is sometimes called the energy from that called the *libido*, or the *libido*, I've heard it pronounced, and the libido is this life force which is largely made up of sexual energy. Now that shocked people when he said that. You have to picture the times; we are talking the late 1800s, the Victorian age in Vienna, Austria, where women were dressed with their colors going up to their necks and their skirts down to their shoes. People would certainly never even talk about sex in polite society in those days and here was Freud suggesting that a newborn baby is a bundle of sexual and aggressive energy. You can imagine people's shock at that. In fact, this fellow Breuer, who he had originally started a practice with, eventually became so uncomfortable with the notion that sex was so important that he dissociated himself from Freud and went his own way. But for Freud this was very important, this life force that was energizing much of our behavior.

Later on, in about the 1920s, Freud published a book that talked about the death instinct as well. This is a bit more controversial, came a little bit later in Freud's career. Freud lived a long time. He lived into the late 1930s and eventually died in London where he had gone the last year of his life because of Nazi persecution. He died of jaw cancer where he had had—you've always seen the picture of Freud with the cigar in his mouth or in his hand in almost every picture—well he got cancer of the jaw and had 33 operations and eventually died of this.

At any rate, Freud made contributions throughout his life, and this death instinct is one of the later contributions. He thought that when life originally came about it was quite tenuous, and there is a life instinct to keep it going, and there was a death instinct that might take it back to being an inanimate object instead of an animate object. The death instinct has stayed with us through evolutionary history into today, and so humans still have some of this death instinct, and that is part of the reason perhaps why people commit suicide. However, usually this death instinct, the life instinct overcomes it, but it is still there, and so at the unconscious level it is seething around trying to figure out what to do—if we cannot kill the owner, let us figure out something else to do—and it leads to aggressive kinds of behavior toward other people. So again he was not a "noble savage" kind of person, he thought that we were all basically quite aggressive and that we had to sort of cap this aggression and hold it down at the unconscious level, and that is part of the source of this kind of conflict that occurs. So all of this is happening at the unconscious level.

Now, he was not the first to actually talk about the unconscious level. Others have done that as well. I was wandering in a bookstore some number of years ago and found a book by Maudsley called, *Body and Mind*. This book was published in 1870. And remember Freud, we are talking about turn of the century here, so this is 25 or 30 years ahead of Freud. And if you look in this book, Maudsley says some things, let me just read just about a paragraph of this book. He says:

The fact that memory is accompanied by consciousness in the supreme centers does not alter the fundamental nature of the organic processes that are the condition of it. The more sure and perfect indeed memory becomes, the more unconscious it becomes and when an idea or mental state has been completely organized, it is reviewed without consciousness and takes its part automatically in our mental operations just as a habitual movement does in our bodily activity. We perceive an operation here the law or organization of conscious acquisitions as unconscious power, which we observed in the functions of the lower nerve centers.

Later he says:

Accordingly in the brain that is not disorganized by injury or disease, your organic registrations are never actually forgotten but endure while life lasts. No wave of oblivion can efface their characters. Consciousness it is true, may be impotent to recall them but a fever or blow on the head, a poison in the blood, a dream, the agony of drowning, the hour of death rending the veil between our present consciousness and these inscriptions, we will sometimes call vividly back in a momentary flash and call back too with all the feelings of the original experience much that seems to have vanished from the mind forever.

So he is talking about the unconscious level there, and that was a revelation to me, but it was not Freud who invented this. In fact, I found another book I was just reading last week in preparation for this lecture on mesmerism from 1892. In this book, I was reading along and they were suddenly talking about the ego. As we will see in a minute, the ego is part of the personality according to Freud, and I thought he made that up. Apparently that was being talked about as well. In science there is a thing called the "zeitgeist," which is a notion that sort of a lot of people had the same kind of thought about the same time, versus a great man theory or great person theory of science which says that one person was responsible for something. This indicates that there was a zeitgeist going on, and Freud was picking up these concepts. And we certainly give him credit for it, but he was not the only one talking about things like unconscious.

Let us talk about the fact that psychoanalytic theory is a deterministic theory. By deterministic, what we mean here is that everything you do is determined, there is a cause for everything you do—not only your actions but also your thoughts and your feelings—that there is a root cause for this. We may not know what the cause is, particularly if it is at the unconscious level, but that in fact is the goal. If we want to change human behavior or change your thoughts or your feelings, we need to understand what the cause was. So, in fact, if you go to the grocery store and you are trying to buy all of the things that you need and you forget the bread, Freud would not say that is an accident or a slip of the mind. He would say there was a reason you forgot the bread; there is no accidents. In fact you may be familiar with the terms "Freudian slip," when people misspeak. Freud would say, well they did not misspeak as an accident, it was not a phonological problem, but there was a deeper problem that was causing this.

There is a story told of a fellow who was a typesetter and typeset the headlines on a newspaper. And this widely decorated general had come back from the war, from the frontlines, and they wrote an article about him, being very positive about him. But the fellow who was doing the typesetting did not think much of this general, and he wrote the headlines and miswrote the headlines and said, "The Battle Scared General Returns From the Front"; it was supposed to be "The Battle Scarred General Returns From the Front." And the newspaper was just very upset about this, and so they printed a retraction the next day and the let the same guy write the headlines unfortunately, and he said, "The Bottle Scarred General Returns From the Front." The point is it was not an accident in the first place. There was a root cause, and that root cause produced the second problem as well. So this is a deterministic kind of thing that everything that you do, that there is a reason for it.

We already talked about how the unconscious is one of the fundamental kinds of things in our society, and that we make a lot of decisions in society as if the unconscious were true. Now beyond that, we want to talk some about the structure of the unconscious and the structure of the personality; and Freud says that there are really three concepts there. Now these are not real entities—you cannot cut open the brain and find the superego over here and the ego over here—but these are concepts that underlie the personality. The first of these is the *id*. The id is said to operate on a pleasure principle; and again we go to the fact that we are not a blank slate, the id is built in. The newborn baby is carrying id around already at birth. So, to the newborn baby, in fact, pleasure is the whole source of what that child wants to do; does not care about anybody else, wants to get all of the milk it can get, wants to get all the pleasure it can get, very hedonistic kind of baby. If we were all id and we are unchecked by any other part of our personality, we would do whatever we wanted to do. There are no wrongs and rights for the id; it just does what feels good. So, if you are sitting there and you like the person's pencil sitting next to you, you think it is better than yours, go ahead and grab it. It is your pencil, it makes you happy, go ahead and take it. Or, if the person sitting next to you is an attractive person, you might grab that person; feels good—that is what the id says to do if unchecked by everything else. You can imagine the chaos in our society if we were all just id. In fact, people who have psychopathologies of various kinds, psychopathic personalities are one way to talk about it, is that they are all id, and they are not properly checked by the other parts of their personality. So it operates on the pleasure principle; it tries to satisfy itself and that is about all we have there. That is built in.

Then shortly after birth our parents start telling us little rules that we have to follow, and other people—our daycare people, television—everybody starts telling us rules. What are the dos and don'ts of life? And that begins to form our conscience, and in psychoanalytic theory that is called the *superego*. So the superego is much like our conscience. It contains all the rules that our parents try to teach us, and it doesn't get along very well with the id, obviously. The id says, "Hey, hey that would be fun, let us go do that." And the superego says, "Oh, no, no, no. That is against the rules, you cannot do that." And the superego has at its disposal a weapon, which is a fairly powerful weapon, and that is guilt. "Go ahead and do that if you want to, but you are going to feel really bad, because I am going to make you feel bad with this guilt if you go do that." Now it is not all bad stuff the superego has, it also has pride and satisfaction if you do the right thing But that guilt is a very powerful kind of thing and keeps the id somewhat in check. It does not make the id happy, but it keeps it in check and that is part of the source of this conflict that is seething at the unconscious level all of the time that we have to deal with, and what Freud was trying to deal with. So that is the superego, sometimes it has to operate on a moral principle. So these are the morals, these are the rules, the dos and don'ts of life.

Now there is a third part of the personality as well, and that is the *ego*. The ego is really required, because if all we had was the id and the superego, and these guys are fighting all the time there, we are going to be very unstable, and sometimes we are going to be over here doing things that give us pleasure and sometimes we are going to be over here feeling really guilty. And so we start to vacillate and swing back and forth and nobody knows what we are going to do from time to time. But the ego comes along, and the ego operates on a reality principle. What is the real world like? What can we get away with? It kind of acts like the referee between the superego and the id, and tries to get them to get along. Again, they are not happy with it, but the ego allows, says "okay, id you want to do this, superego say you cannot do that, what can we do here to settle this, to mediate between these two? What can we do to get some happiness but not break the rules too much either?" So that is a function of the ego.

Now as we get older, the ego gets stronger. Again, the ego is not there from birth; this is something that we learn as we experience the environment, we move around, we learn about reality and what we can get away with and what we cannot get away with, and the ego gets stronger. An ego's strength is a good thing in terms of being a psychological concept. The stronger the ego, the better developed you are as a person, and the stronger your personality is. So after a while, you do not have to mediate every little conflict. What you end up with is sort of an image of who you are.

So I have this image of David Martin in my mind, about what this guy named David Martin does. And whenever I am confronted by something that my id telling me, "Boy, it would be great to go do that, wouldn't it?" And my superego saying, "Well, you know that is really kind of against the rules." I have this picture of who I am that I compare these things to and say, what would David Martin do in this case? And as I get a stronger ego, a stronger self-image, that picture gets stronger, and that allows me to be much more consistent in my behavior. So I now can solve this problem and at least outwardly appear that things are fairly placid, even though at the unconscious level again things are not so placid. There are still these seething kinds of forces against one another caused by the life instinct and the death instinct that are sort of fighting with each other; the death instinct that cannot kill the organisms, so that the death instinct is causing aggression; and then you have the id who wants to use this aggression to go against other people to feel good; and you have the superego saying, "no you cannot do that," and will give you a lot of guilt; and you have the ego trying to referee this whole sort of mess that is going on down there at the same time. So you can imagine the kinds of problems that you have at the unconscious level.

So that was Freud's conception of this whole thing and what is going on, and if you have all of these problems at the unconscious level, and you have all of these conflicts, how are you going to solve the problems? And that is where he came up with the basic tenets of psychoanalysis; with psychoanalysis, with things like free association, with dream analysis, with some projective tests and that kind of thing. What the whole purpose of that was to break through this censoring mechanism and try to be able to get down there at the unconscious level, and from time to time get a little inkling; you could never be sure what is down there, but you get inklings about this. And that is why psychoanalysis takes such a long time, because you just get little bits and pieces from time to time and try to build what is at the unconscious level to understand these conflicts that are going on down there. So it is quite a complex problem to try to figure out what is going on at the unconscious level.

Now we have been over the rudiments today of psychoanalysis, but it goes into more detail as well. There are certain stages; it is a theory that has developmental stages to it, as you can imagine, because we start out as an id—that would be a different stage than after we add little superego to it and a little ego to it, and so we have these psychosexual developmental stages. We will talk more about that in the next lecture. We will also talk more about how you deal with the kinds of conflicts that are going on at the unconscious level, because these conflicts at the unconscious level are quite upsetting to the person. We would have to have ways of coping with these kinds of conflicts; and we do that, and we call then "defense mechanisms." We will talk a little bit about that in the next lecture as well.

So, today I have given you a little background in terms of whom Sigmund Freud was, how he came up with the notion of the unconscious, how important the unconscious was to psychoanalytic theory and also to our thinking about how our social institutions work. It is really the underpinnings of a lot of the ways we designed our social systems. And we have also talked some about the parts of our unconscious and our personality and how they are in constant conflict. So next time, we will go into a little bit more detail about this. Thank you.

Lecture Six
Details of Psychoanalytic Theory

Scope:

Psychoanalytic theory proposes that psychosexual energy is focused on various anatomical parts during a series of developmental stages. During the oral stage, the energy is on activities of the mouth, such as eating, and insufficient gratification can lead to oral fixations, including overeating. During the anal stage, the focus is on toilet training, and fixations can lead to compulsive or slovenly behaviors. During the phallic stage, the focus is on dominance and aggressive activities, and fixation can involve undue competitiveness. During the genital phase, sharing, caring, mature relationships can occur. Boys go through an Oedipus conflict in which, unconsciously, they would like to sexually possess their mothers, but the father is in the way and might castrate them. This is resolved in the latent period, when boys learn to behave like dad in order to attract someone like mom. Girls discover they are missing a part and have penis envy, which leads them to want to possess dad or a boy child. During the latent period, they learn to act like mom as a wife and mother. Defense mechanisms are unconscious ways that we lie to ourselves to protect our psyches. These include: repression, rationalization, and projection. Some would argue that Freud's theory has outlived its usefulness in today's world, while others assert that parts of the theory are still applicable and that Freud's writings are valuable from a philosophical and literary point of view.

Outline

I. Psychoanalytic theory is a developmental theory and proposes that a person's psychosexual energy, called the *libido*, is cathected, or focused, on various anatomical parts; this process produces stages of development of the personality.

   A. In the earliest stage, the *oral stage*, energy is focused on the mouth, and oral activities give the most pleasure.

      1. Especially during the first year of life, the baby is active in seeking out food and engaging in other oral activities, such as thumb sucking and teething.

2. If oral gratification is not sufficient, the person can get fixated on the oral stage, which might lead to such later-life activities as overeating, compulsive smoking, nail biting, and so on.

B. The second stage, the *anal stage*, occurs at ages 2 to 4, and the energy is fixated on the anus.

1. During the anal stage, the child derives pleasure from anal activities, particularly those associated with toilet training.

2. If parents are too strict with toilet training, an anal compulsive fixation can occur, which in later life might be manifested in such behaviors as compulsive neatness.

3. If parents are too lenient in toilet training, the person might in later life be slovenly and disorganized.

C. The third stage is the *phallic stage*, occurring about ages 3 to 5, in which the energy is focused on the (male) genitals.

1. During the phallic stage, energy is focused on the genitals, at least in little boys, and pleasure is derived from masturbatory behaviors and in behaviors related to dominance and aggression.

2. In the phallic stage, little boys begin to play aggressive games, such as war and king-of-the-hill, and to show dominance.

3. A fixation in the phallic stage can lead to adult behavior that overemphasizes competitiveness and treats women as trophies.

D. After the third stage is the *latent period*, which is not really a stage and will be discussed later in this lecture.

E. The last stage is called the *genital stage* and occurs around the time of puberty.

1. During the genital stage, energy is still focused on the genitals, but the focus is on developing caring/sharing relationships with significant others (of the opposite sex, according to Freud).

2. According to Freud, one cannot develop full maturity as a person unless the genital stage is achieved.

II. During the phallic stage and into the latent period, Freud proposed that some complex dynamics occur and that these dynamics are different for boys than for girls.

A. During the phallic stage, when little boys are engaging in competitive activities and looking for prizes to be won, at the unconscious level, they discover that mom is the biggest prize and have yearnings to possess her sexually. This is called the *Oedipus conflict*.

  1. An obvious impediment to the little boy's desire for his mother is his father.

  2. At the unconscious level, the boy is afraid of his dad even to the point that, if his desire were known, dad might castrate him; this fear causes castration anxiety.

  3. The resolution of this Oedipus conflict—the desire for mom with the fear of dad—is that the boy resolves to be like dad so that he can attract someone like mom.

  4. The boy begins to behave like dad, and the latent period is needed to give the boy sufficient time to learn the sex-typed behavior to be like dad.

B. During the phallic stage, the little girl discovers she is missing an anatomical part and develops *penis envy*.

  1. Her unconscious tells her that one way she can gain this missing part is to possess dad sexually; thus, she develops the female equivalent of the Oedipus conflict, sometimes called the *Electra conflict*.

  2. A second way she could get a penis is to have a boy child.

  3. Because mom is in the way, preventing her from possessing dad and having a child, she resolves the Electra conflict by deciding to become like mom, both as a wife and as a mother, and uses the latency period to learn the sex-typing that allows her to do this.

III. Because there is so much conflict present in the personality, such as the conflict among the id, superego, and ego, our personalities have developed unconscious ways of defending ourselves against the anxiety generated by conflict.

A. The way we deal with this anxiety is to use what are called *defense mechanisms*, which are lies we tell ourselves at the unconscious level.

   1. Freud proposed a number of defense mechanisms, one of the most important of which is *repression*. This mechanism is used to keep unacceptable thoughts, feelings, and memories at an unconscious level and prevent these from reaching consciousness.

   2. A second widely used defense mechanism is *rationalization*, which makes unacceptable and irrational behaviors appear rational.

   3. *Projection* is a third defense mechanism, in which we deny our unacceptable characteristics and assign, or project, them onto other people.

B. Although some might argue that all defense mechanisms are bad because they are dishonest, others assert that when used in moderation, defense mechanisms lead to positive mental health outcomes.

   1. A way to illustrate defense mechanisms is to draw a continuum from bad to good and have people indicate where on that continuum they fall.

   2. The fact that the vast majority of people place themselves in the upper half ("good") of that continuum shows the power of defense mechanisms.

IV. Some psychologists today would argue that Freud's psychoanalytic theory has worn out its usefulness and is no longer relevant, while others maintain that there is still some usefulness to the theory.

A. Mikita Brottman argues that most psychologists consider Freud's theories to be absolutely irrelevant to modern science, but non-psychologists think that he is a valuable writer, theorist, and philosopher, much like Marx or Hegel.

B. Linda Peterson has written a tongue-in-cheek feminist version of psychoanalytic theory, proposing that little boys have vagina envy, which illustrates that the theory is largely semantic and not data-based.

C. I would argue that the concept of the unconscious has been quite valuable to modern society and still has social relevance.

D. It may also be the case that if one gets rid of the controversial anatomical names for the developmental stages, there may still be some validity to the concepts involved.

Essential Reading:

Sigmund Freud, *Introductory Lectures on Psychoanalysis.*

Supplementary Reading:

Mikita Brottman, "The Two Freuds," *The Chronicle of Higher Education*, July 9, 2004, p. B5.

Questions to Consider:

1. How would you go about collecting scientifically defensible evidence for the existence of Freud's psychosexual stages of development?

2. Do you think that psychoanalytic theory offers a language and conceptual structure that helps you understand behaviors and events in your life?

Lecture Six—Transcript
Details of Psychoanalytic Theory

In the last lecture, we talked about some of the fundamentals of psychoanalytic theory, introduced you to Freud, said how important the unconscious is in our behavior and how there is a lot of conflict going on at the unconscious level, and there is also a lot of different energy forces that are moving at the unconscious level, at least according to Freud. We also talked about some of the parts of our personality including the id, sort of the basic part that operates under the pleasure principle; the ego that operated under the reality principle; and the superego that operates under a moral principle.

Freud's theory is more than just a static theory. As we grow older, we go through developmental stages. During these stages we have this energy that I talked about last time, this libido, this sexual aggressive energy that gets focused on various anatomical parts, according to Freud, depending upon our particular age. So I want to go over those stages today with you and I also want to talk some about defense mechanisms. If you will recall, we said that there was a great deal of conflict at the unconscious level, and we have to sort of protect ourselves from this conflict; and the way we do it is through defense mechanisms. So we will talk some about that. And finally, in this lecture, we will wrap up by talking about the usefulness of psychoanalytic theory today. Is there anything useful about it today? So we will consider some of those topics at the end of the lecture.

Let us go to the developmental part of psychoanalytic theory; and we have various stages of development. In these stages of development, we have the psychosexual energy that is focused on various anatomical parts, and that is where they get the names for these various stages. The earliest stage is the *oral stage* and this psychosexual energy is focused on the mouth and on mouthy activities. During the oral stage, during the time it is focused on the mouth, certain things become important, like eating activities, other mouthy activities; you will find children with things that they manufacture to stick into their mouths in place of their thumbs. And you cannot stop kids from sticking their thumbs in their mouth; they have got their thumbs in their mouths before they are even born. But, they also have things like teething rings and other kinds of things that they can derive pleasure from these kinds of activities with their mouths.

The general notion in these stages is that you derive pleasure from the stage, and if you derive sufficient pleasure, at a certain point you move on to the next stage. It is required that you derive this pleasure in order to move on. If you do not you might get hung up in a particular stage, you might get fixated in a particular stage and not move on to the next. In fact, initially Freud said it was impossible to move on to the next if you get fixated. Later he softened that position a little bit and said that you can move on in certain ways, but leave some of your behaviors behind in the earlier stages as well.

As I go through the stages, we will talk a little bit about what happens if you get fixated in that stage. So you have this little kid, who is concerned about mouthy activities, especially eating. And you do not have to teach the kid; they are born with reflexes to root for the mother's nipple, and then once they get the mother's nipple, to suckle on it. You do not have to teach them that kind of thing, they already have that mouthy activity built right into them. If they get enough to eat and they are satisfied with their mouthy activities, they will move on to the next stage. But if they are not, they may get hung up to some extent, at least in the oral stage; and that can be shown by a number of different possible fixations. Somebody who does not get enough to eat for example, it might show up in later over concern with eating activities and lead to obesity, lead to eating too much; lead to perhaps eating disorders like bulimia and anorexia, that sort of thing. They all have to do with mouth and eating activities.

So that is one way that you might find somebody—at least according to Freud—that would be a reason, an explanation, and a cause for these kinds of behaviors. It also might show up in certain kinds of leftover mouthy functions. Back about 20 years ago, I had smoked pipe for about 15 years, and smoking a pipe back in those days, lots of professors did that. And so I smoked a pipe, and probably half the time I had the pipe in my mouth, it was not even lit. I just enjoyed having that pipe in my mouth. It allowed me to do mouthy kinds of things. Today I use a toothpick sometimes in the same way. When I am lecturing on this in a large classroom, I will usually look around at about this point in the lecture and see three or four students with their pencils in their mouths. And I say ah ha, there you go; you are still hung up to some extent in the oral phase. So eating too much, smoking too much. Freud, if he were around today might argue that smoking was part of this, and in fact, as I mentioned in the last lecture, Freud smoked a cigar himself and it caused him all sorts of health problems. So smoking too much—perhaps even talking too much—that is a mouthy activity. Probably most professors are hung up to some extent in the oral stage, at least according to Freud, because of the amount that they talk.

Assuming you have gotten through this stage and have the proper satisfaction in this stage, you would then move on to the next stage. The first stage would have occurred during the first year of life and into the second year of life. At about this time, with proper satisfaction, the energy becomes cathected or focused on the other end of the gastrointestinal tract, on the anus. It is called the *anal stage*. This stage occurs during the second year and into the third year of life, and it varies a bit depending upon certain kinds of conditions. During the anal stage there may be a certain amount of pleasure that is derived from the actual physiological activity of elimination, but there is also pleasure derived because it is the first time you have to follow somebody else's rules. Because what happens during this time, if you look around, you will see that toilet training occurs during this time. So anal activities become very important in terms of toilet training. And somebody now imposes some rules on this otherwise wonderful kind of existence that you have led up until this time. You have to do certain things at the right time, in the right way, and if you do so, you can get pleasured because you have satisfied somebody else.

Now things can go wrong in this phase also. So in this stage you can have a situation where your parents are too concerned about getting it exactly right, so they impose this—it is a particular time, it is two years of age, everybody is ready to toilet train at two years of age, whether or not your are physiologically ready. Here is how you do it—they set up the whole situation in a very particular way. According to Freud, if this happens and there is over-emphasis on sort of the details of it, a person might end up being obsessive compulsive about things, and we call somebody anal that way. That is directly out of psychoanalytic theory. You accuse somebody of being anal, you are saying that what happened during the anal stage is that there is too much emphasis on all of these details.

It could go the other way too. If there is not emphasis on that, according to Freud, you might end up being kind of a slovenly person. You look around, and this person, you walk into their house and there are things stacked all over and stacks of clothing over in the corner that need washing; and all of this would be an indication of slovenly behavior that is left over from the anal stage too. So that is what happens, and there are even more symbolic things, like smearing someone else metaphorically, through things like gossip; and Freud might say that is a symbolic way of still being in the anal stage. Assuming you got through that stage okay, and you derived appropriate pleasure, you would move on to the third stage, which is named the phallic stage.

The *phallic stage* occurs around three year to about five years. You will notice here in the beginning of the fact that Freud sometimes gave women not their proper due, because this is named after a male anatomical part, not a female anatomical part. So this energy gets cathected or focused on the genitalia, and for little boys, this becomes very important for activities that have to do with dominance activities. It is true that some of it may be some masturbatory activity, for example; but also it has to do with activities that are aggressive. Perhaps this is from our last lecture where we were talking about the death instinct and how that leads to aggression. In this case there is aggression, and this aggression seems to be moving toward competition and trying to establish where you are in the dominance hierarchy of life. So you see little boys who are playing with guns and swords, sort of symbolic phallic symbols in this case. You see little boys playing games like King of the Hill; I am bigger better than you are, kind of more powerful; I am up here and you are down here kinds of games. So this phallic stage is very important during this period of time for little boys.

For little girls, something slightly different is happening, and we will talk about that in a few minutes when we talk about the latent phase. So for the little boys at this point, they are playing these aggressive games, and they can get fixated in this stage as well. If they do not get enough satisfaction in this stage, that would be manifest perhaps later on in somebody who is too overly competitive for example. The

45-year-old guy that is still out there on the basketball court throwing elbows and trying to prove that he is a super jock when he is well past his prime; and that would be an indication that somebody is hung up in the phallic stage still. Or perhaps in his profession—the stockbroker; he wants the biggest portfolio around; or he is an architect and wants to build the most magnificent and tallest building around. All of these would be indications that he is hung up in the phallic stage to some extent.

Another indication is the way that men treat women. And in this stage, women are prizes to be won, they are trophies; we even have language for that, a "trophy wife" for example. This person is a trophy, and we also have a language for what goes on here—"Did you score last night?" I mean, this sounds like a game doesn't it? We are trying to treat women as objects in the phallic stage. In fact the whole word game has recently come back into vogue; do you have game? Can you play the field and have some success with that sort of thing with women? So, in fact, if women are being treated as objects that would be some indication that the male is still in the phallic stage. Toward the end of the phallic stage, something happens, but I do not want to great detail now. It causes what is sometimes called a "latent period," and I'll come back and talk about why that is.

Once that period goes by then it is possible to move into the final stage and that is the *genital stage*. In the genital stage, we still have the energy cathected on the genitalia, but it is in a very different way; it is no longer a competitive way. At this stage, which was Freud's final stage—and he gets some criticisms for that because it seems unusual; this stage occurs about the time of puberty, the genital stage. And to say that the person is fully formed and mature right at puberty seems to be a stretch. To claim that we do not, through the rest of our lives, have psychosexual stages going on seems to be something of a criticism of Freud. At any rate, in the genital stage, what we now have is the ability to form a sharing, caring kind of relationship with somebody else, so that we have a sort of more permanent—the woman is now not an object, but in fact a partner in an enterprise. An intimacy develops that allows this kind of relationship. And that is the genital stage that occurs during about the time of puberty, if you have successfully negotiated all of these other stages.

Now let me go back a minute and talk about one of the more entertaining aspects of psychoanalytic theory, and this one—some people—I have trouble lecturing about this with quite a straight face, but let me do it anyway. In the phallic stage, let us go back to that and let us take the little boy. The little boy is interested in competition; interested in winning the biggest prizes. Women are prizes to be won; who would be the biggest prize to win? Well, the most important woman in his life, his mom. So at the unconscious level—let us get this right, this is the unconscious level—we do not have this little boy scheming to go out on a date with mom and get her into bed or something like that. But indeed, what Freud said— and this was shocking to people—was at the unconscious level, the little boy does want to sexually possess mom. He does want to go bed with mom. And that is a desire; he has to win mom in this way.

But there is a problem, of course, and the problem is dad. Dad is in the way. Dad already has mom and he knows he cannot quite get by dad. Dad is a big guy, and on top of that, Dad may castrate him. And so he has castration anxiety from dad. So dad is in the way and he cannot do this. This is a conflict. Sometimes called the "oedipal conflict"—or the "oedipal complex," it is sometimes called that as well—after a Greek tragedy where Oedipus Rex, as a young man, went to a foreign land and then came back and fell in love with this older woman, and ended up having a relationship with her and then later found out it was his mom, at which point he poked his eyes out and other kinds of… the usual things that happen in Greek tragedies.

So this is named after Oedipus Rex. It is called the Oedipal conflict. So this is the conflict: they would like to possess mom, dad is in the way; what is he going to do here? Well, we have written songs about that kind of thing. "I want a gal just like the gal who married dear old dad." Well, he cannot have mom, so he wants a gal just like the gal who married dear old dad. How does he get a gal like the gal that married dear old dad? To act like dad, dad was successful at doing this. So, in fact, he can act like dad in order to accomplish this. So he ends up learning to walk like dad and talk like dad and do things the way dad does; what is sometimes called "sex typing." He learns appropriate behavior for his sex so that he can accomplish the getting of somebody like mom, since he cannot have mom.

So this latent phase take a certain amount of time to do. You will remember that the phallic stage, we said, is over at about five years of age, when this Oedipal conflict is resolved. And then you have to have this period of time, up until puberty, for all of this learning to occur; for the little boy to learn to act like dad so he can have somebody like mom.

Now what happens to the little girl? This is all boy related here. Well the little girl at this point, according to Freud, looks around, and she discovers that she is missing something; she is missing an anatomical part. She does not have a penis and so she has what is "penis envy," according to Freud; again, quite a controversial kind of concept. And so she feels incomplete without this penis; and so how is she going to get this? Well, dad has one, so it is kind of a similar situation, a parallel situation with the little boy; because dad has one, so she would like to possess dad, but she cannot because mom is in the way and that is a conflict. This is called the "Elektra conflict" for the little girl, after another character in a play that had a similar sort of thing that Oedipus Rex; so it is the Elektra conflict. She can get somebody like dad by acting like mom as a wife and a lover. But she can also get a penis by having a child, so she can have a boy child who has one of these, and so she can also act like mom—not just as a wife, but also as a mother. So during this latent phase for her, from the end of the phallic stage until puberty and the genital stage, she watches mom, acts like mom, tries to act like a wife, and tries to act like a mother. That is sort of the inner workings here of these stages, and people find that sort of unusual and a bit bizarre when they first hear those things.

Let us move on to a slightly different topic. We will come back and talk about stages just a little bit at the end of lecture. Let us move on and talk some about defense mechanisms. Again, if we go back to the first lecture on psychoanalytic theory, what we ended up with was an unconscious level where we had all this seething kind of activity going on, because we had the death wish and we had the life instinct that were sort of fighting with each other to try to gain control of the personality; and we had the id that was trying to operate on a pleasure principle completely unchecked by other parts of the personality an instinctual kind of thing. Then we had the superego that was like our conscience that contained all the rules and was fighting with the id. And we had the ego that was trying to referee this whole big mess, and through self-image and some other ways, tried to mediate here. But nevertheless, we end up with a great deal of conflict at the unconscious level, and the conflict sort of gets in the way of a good self-image. So, in fact, if we want to be mentally healthy, one thing that we need to do is develop ways of coping with all of this conflict that is going on.

Freud suggested that we do this, again at the unconscious level, lying to ourselves a little bit, basically, and having certain kinds of mechanisms to defend our sense of worth from all of this stuff that is going on at the unconscious level; and he called these defense mechanisms. Now he had a whole bunch of these defense mechanisms, I just want to talk about three of these as illustrative of the kinds of defense mechanisms he was talking about.

The first one that I will mention is repression. With repression, again if you picture the iceberg we had last time, where above the waterline the conscious level and below the waterline the unconscious level, what repression does is use this censoring mechanism at the waterline to push down and hold down everything at the unconscious level. So we have certain thoughts and feelings that we have a difficult time dealing with, and so they do not enter into our conscious level; they are pushed down. It does not mean that they do not cause problems; they can still cause us some problems. At least at the conscious level, we feel pretty good because we do not have to deal with all of this conflict that is seething down at the unconscious level. We keep it repressed; we keep it pushed down at that level.

A second and widely used one is rationalization. With rationalization—in fact some would argue that that is the main function of the conscious level, is to rationalize the way we were behaving, when in fact the cause of the way were behaving is derived at the unconscious level, and what our conscious level does is run around looking at our behavior and trying to come up with excuses for why we behave the way we did. That is rationalization. We can lie to ourselves a number of ways. We can lie to ourselves about, for example, suppose you have a goal you want to reach and you cannot reach that goal. One way to lie to yourself is to say well the goal was not worth anything anyway, sort of Aesop's fable about the fox that was jumping up and trying to grab the grapes and they were too high for him to get them, and he stalked off saying they were probably sour anyway. So we say that the goal was not worth it. We have rationalized that. Or perhaps we rationalize a particular barrier that is keeping us from getting to a goal. So, that barrier, we blame on other people—that barrier—instead of blaming it on our own inadequacies to keep us from reaching the goal. So there are a number of ways you can employ rationalization as a defense mechanism.

The third one is projection, where you project some characteristic about yourself on somebody else and attribute it to him or her instead of to yourself. There is a kind of cute piece of research that was done on a fraternity. They went in and had all of the fraternity brothers rate themselves on such things as: How generous or stingy am I? How friendly or unfriendly am I? And they rated their fraternity brothers as well. Then they went in and they found that, for a lot of people, they discovered that perhaps one person was rated as fairly stingy. So they then went to look at the person's ratings and he rated himself as being quite generous but rated most of the other people as quite stingy. He projected this characteristic of himself onto the other people. So this is another defense mechanism. Again, these are all, let me remind you, at the unconscious level. We are not doing this, we are not thinking devious thoughts at the conscious level and making up stories and that sort of thing. All of these are happening at the unconscious level.

There are others like intellectualization, sublimation, and some other defense mechanisms that you might have heard of. Now are these good or are these bad? Are these good for you or bad for you, and how effective are they? I do a little exercise in my class to try to illustrate this. I say imagine a continuum, and on one end of the continuum is bad—this is the worst person you can imagine; this person is not smart, they are devious, ugly, slimiest character you can image. The other end, imagine good—that is the best person; an honest person, smart, friendly, the best person you can imagine. And now what I want you to do, I tell my students, is put yourself on this continuum somewhere. Put a mental checkmark on this continuum as where you think you are.

Now I am going to keep it simple, I am just going to bisect this continuum right in the middle and I want you to decide whether your check mark was on the good end of the continuum or the bad end of the continuum. I tell them to all close their eyes and I say that I am not going to do this until I see every eye closed here and then I want you to hold up your hand and tell me whether you are on the good end of the continuum or the bad end of the continuum. So everybody closes his or her eyes and I say, "Quickly hold up your hand." I look around, and then, "Okay, on the bad end at the continuum hold up your hand." And after they do that, I tell them, "Okay open your eyes."

I said, I just counted, and there were three people out of this class of 200 who were in the lower half of the continuum. Three people. I said now this is an exceptional class probably, but surely, we have more than three people who, if reality were to hold sway, would be in the lower half of the continuum. Why do most of you think that you are in the upper half of the continuum? I think it is because you employed defense mechanisms, and you do so rather well. I say I think that is probably a good thing, because I think that defense mechanisms, I would sure rather deal with people in life who think well of themselves then people who think badly of themselves. So I think from a mental health point of view, it is probably a good idea as long as you do not over employ these. Because if you employ these to too great an extent, that is almost the definition of mental illness. If you lie to yourself such that there is break with reality, that in fact is a definition of psychosis, as we will see later on. So, when employed in sort of in a normal way, this is probably a good thing, defense mechanisms.

Finally, let us talk a little bit about the usefulness for today's world of Freud's psychoanalytic theory. I mentioned in the last lecture that some of my colleagues wonder why I even talk about this anymore because they see very little usefulness. And the major reason they say little usefulness is that they do not believe it has any scientific credentials. We talk about it as a theory, but in fact, in some respects, it is an almost untestable theory. How do you refute it? How do you say, no there is not such a thing as repression? Or how do you say, no there is not just these three parts of the personality; there is another part? How do you test that? How do you run an experiment? It is not a scientific theory. It is really a way of talking about things, more of a language, and maybe if we accept it at that level, that maybe we are better off. In fact, Mikita Brottman, in an article I just read about a half-year ago, was arguing that Freud is still valuable, but not so much to psychologists any more. That, in fact, writers, theorists, and philosophers still like Freud a lot, and they quote him a lot—much like they do Marx or Hegel—and consider him sort of a philosophy point of a view, not a scientific point of view. He was also an excellent writer, and people appreciate that about Freud too. So maybe there is something there in terms of our thought about people and what human nature is like, even if there is not too much scientific basis to it.

Linda Peterson wrote a tongue-in-cheek article a few years ago about Freud, and let me just mention some of this article. She talks about how women have the mystery of birth and how this is a wondrous event, and how man has gazed in wonder at the mystery of birth and the new child, and they are in awe that the woman has this power and fortitude to bring forth a new life. And they have an envy that is the result of this and that envy is an envy called "vagina envy"—this sounds a little familiar doesn't it?—and that so they envy the fact women can bring children into the world, and little boys are in awe of this and they wish to accomplish something different, something that their poor organ cannot accomplish. And so, in the man there is a sense of being incomplete, a lack of inner self. So, they have this vagina envy, and this results in things like little boys wanting to have pockets in their pants and businessmen having pockets all over, in their shirts and pants, and all of this in vagina envy.

She is doing this somewhat tongue-in-cheek of course, and pointing out the fact that there is not much scientific basis to psychoanalytic theory, and you can change the language and use it the other way around to justify other kinds of concepts, and that there is no way of refuting that. Just like there is no way in refuting penis envy, there is probably no way of refuting vagina envy either.

Is there anything in psychoanalytic theory for us? I think I pointed out last time that I think the most important thing in psychoanalytic theory is the whole notion of unconscious, because we do use unconscious in building our social institutions, and I think that is a very important residual concept from it; and nearly everyone believes that, and that is a basic tenet of this theory. It is also probably true that if you got rid of the anatomical names, we could even find some validity in the various stages. Indeed, I could argue that the first stage should be probably not, we would not call it an oral stage, but let us call it almost a survival stage. You have to learn how to survive when you are a kid; how to keep from choking, how to get enough food in you to survive. And it is a very sort of individual thing. And then, up to a point that works, but then you have to learn to follow somebody else's rules. Let us not call it the anal stage, but let us call it sort of picking up on other people's rules. So somebody says you have to do this, and you have to learn how to do that. And then the third stage, lets not call it the phallic stage, but let us call it a socialization stage, let us say where you have to learn not only the rules of one other person, but now you have to learn the rules of society. Where do I fit in to that?

Finally, you probably, at some point, in order to be a mature individual, have to have the capability of developing an intimate relationship with somebody as well. So if we get rid of the anatomical names, perhaps even that has some validity to it. So now we have been over the various parts of psychoanalytic theory, and you can take it for what it is worth at this point. If you find it useful as a language, to talk about things, then I am glad that I told you something about it. Thank you.

Lecture Seven
Classification of Mental Illnesses

Scope:

The definition of abnormal behavior is multidimensional, a mixture of various criteria for determining whether a behavior pattern is normal. It is somewhat subjective and can change over time. Some of the criteria that can be used in this determination include the following: whether the behavior is statistically rare, whether the behavior violates social and moral norms, whether the behavior is so unpredictable that it causes safety concerns, and whether the behavior causes unhappiness. People have been trying to classify mental illness from the time of Hippocrates (400 B.C.) until today (DSM-IV–TR™). Today's system has increased its reliability by focusing on observable behaviors, rather than underlying theoretically based constructs. The system also has multiple axes that evaluate not only the clinical condition of a person but also whether the person has a personality disorder or mental retardation, whether there is a medical condition present, whether there are life stressors, and whether the person functions at a satisfactory level. In any particular year, more than 18% of the U.S. population will have mental disorders, with the most frequent being anxiety disorder (12%), substance abuse (6%), mood disorder (5%), and schizophrenia (1%).

Outline

I.   Many criteria can be used to determine whether a person's behavior is normal or abnormal and whether the person has a mental disorder.

   A. One criterion is whether the person's behavior is statistically deviant, although this criterion by itself is not sufficient for inferring mental illness; for example, geniuses are rare, but that does not mean they are mentally ill.

   B. Another criterion is whether the person is violating the moral and social standards of society enough that it makes others uncomfortable. For example, exhibitionists may be of no danger to others, but they make us uncomfortable.

C. Another criterion is whether the behavior is so unpredictable that we are unsure whether the person exhibiting the behavior may harm him- or herself or others.

D. A final criterion is whether the person is unhappy with his or her condition.

E. In most states and provinces, for a person to be committed to a mental facility, he or she must have a mental illness and must be of potential harm to others or to himself or herself.

II. Classification and treatment of mental disorders has a long history.

    A. What is the advantage of classifying mental illness?

        1. The treatment depends on the classification.

        2. An additional reason is that health insurance payments depend on the classification.

        3. A disadvantage of classification is that it can become a self-fulfilling prophesy.

    B. We know from archeological digs that mental disorders were apparently treated by trephining, the process of chipping a hole in the skull.

    C. Hippocrates (460–377 B.C.), the father of medicine, offered the first classification of mental disorders, into three categories: mania, melancholia, and phrenitis (brain fever).

    D. From the Islamic tradition, Avicenna from Arabia (c. 980–1037) added epilepsy and hysteria to the list of disorders.

    E. Not much progress was made in the classification of mental illnesses through the Middle Ages and even up to the 20th century. Throughout this time, mental illness was considered to be caused by possession by demons.

    F. Although some work was done on the classification of mental illnesses in the early part of the 20th century, a formal classification system was not introduced until 1952, when the *Diagnostic and Statistical Manual of Mental Disorders* (DSM-I) was introduced in an attempt to standardize classification of soldiers from World War II.

G. Since the original DSM, there have been several revisions, leading to today's DSM-IV–TR™, which is more observation-based rather than theory-based.

III. In the next several lectures, we will use DSM-IV–TR™ to help us look at the major mental illnesses.

A. DSM-IV–TR™ actually has five axes on which people are classified, and a thorough diagnosis includes an evaluation of each of the axes.

1. Axis I lists all the possible clinical syndromes that may be the focus of clinical attention, such as schizophrenia and bipolar disorder.

2. Axis II contains personality disorders and mental retardation that a person may have in addition to a clinical syndrome.

3. Axis III is an evaluation of the person's general medical condition, such as having chronic pain or diabetes.

4. Axis IV evaluates psychosocial and environmental stressors that may have contributed to the person's problem.

5. Axis V is a global assessment of how the person is functioning at the current time.

B. Before looking in detail at the various mental disorders, it might be helpful to get some idea of the prevalence of the major types of disorders, using a recent study (Little, 2002) that estimated the 12-month prevalence of major disorders, excluding personality disorders.

1. Mental illness affects more than 37 million adults in America during a given year, or about 18.5% of the population.

2. Anxiety disorders affect nearly 12% of the population.

3. Mood disorders (such as depression and bipolar disorder) affect a little more than 5% of the population.

4. Substance-abuse disorders, including alcohol and drug abuse, affect about 6% of the population.

5. Schizophrenia affects about 1% of the population.

Essential Reading:

James Butcher, Susan Mineka, and Jill Hooley, *Abnormal Psychology*, 12th ed., chapters 1, 2, and 4.

Supplementary Reading:

American Psychiatric Association, *Diagnostic and Statistical Manual of Mental Disorders*, 4th ed.

Questions to Consider:

1. For the following disorders, which of the criteria mentioned in item I above would be primary in determining whether the disorder was abnormal: depression, mental retardation, schizophrenia, and/or voyeurism (peeping)?

2. Do you think there are clear boundaries between the various classifications of mental disorders, or do you think that there are continua of behaviors with no clear boundaries?

Lecture Seven—Transcript
Classification of Mental Illnesses

At this point in this lecture we want to begin to talk about mental illnesses a little bit. It is a very important part of psychology, as I mentioned in the very first lecture. Clinical psychology comprises about two-thirds of what psychologists do. Those people are concerned with folks who have problems, and these problems are mental problems, and we need to somehow figure out what kind of problem they have and then try to do something with them. That is what we are going to be talking about in the next series of lectures.

Today we are going to talk about first how we know abnormal behavior when we see it. What makes it distinct from normal behavior? Where do you draw the line? Secondly, today we will then talk about classifications systems that have been suggested. How do you classify the various mental illnesses? What are the distinctions among these mental illnesses? So we will talk some about classification systems, and finally, we will talk some about the prevalence of sort of the various overall major classifications of disorders, how prevalent they are in our society, how many folks have these disorders.

So let us begin by considering how we know abnormal behavior when we see it. Suppose I were standing up here and I took off my shoe and I walked back here to the wall and started slamming my shoe on the wall. They would probably fire me from the job I have here, but what would you think out there? Would you think that I am abnormal? Probably. Do you think I ought to be locked up for that behavior? Well, maybe, maybe not. We will talk a little bit more about that. Or suppose instead, that instead of wearing this shirt and tie, I came in this morning with a trench coat on and started my lecture and about this point in the lecture unbutton my trench coat and open it up and I did not have any clothes on underneath. Now, am I normal or abnormal at that point in your eyes? Is that abnormal behavior? Should you lock me up for that? Suppose instead that I wore a dress in here today. Had a nice skirt and a dress on in here. Would you think I am abnormal? Would you lock me up for that?

All of these are sort of questions about where do we draw the line. How do we know abnormal behavior when we see it? There have been numerous criteria to try to decide what is normal and what is abnormal. And people employ these in a rather loose way sometime and mix these criteria. For example, you could define abnormality in a statistical way. If you have a distribution, you have some characteristic along the bottom of that distribution, and then you plot the number of cases of people along that characteristic, a frequency count. You would end up with a distribution—you are probably familiar with things like bell shaped curves—and then we can sort of say the tails of that distribution are by definition abnormal. They are not what most people are. They are deviant in some ways; they are statistically deviant. We have terms like standard deviation, which is talking about deviation from some norm that we expect to have in behavior. So we can say that the people on the tails are deviant; does that make them mentally ill?

Well suppose this was plotting some form of intelligence, IQ score, or something like that. Suppose I told you I have an IQ of 140 (do not I wish); if I had an IQ of 140, would you consider me abnormal? Well, I do not know. Would you consider me mentally ill? Probably not. We would say, hey that is great; got an IQ that high. Suppose I said I had an IQ of 64. So I am way down on the other end, that other tail. Am I abnormal? Statistically I would be defined as abnormal. Am I mentally ill? Actually, we will see as we go through this classification system that we are about to talk about. Yes, I do have some form of mental illness, a mental retardation when I have an IQ measure down there. So on one end of the scale we called it perhaps abnormal, but we certainly did not call it mental illness. And on the other end, we did call it mental illness. So, statistically it may work some of the time but it certainly does not work all of the time. Is Lance Armstrong abnormal? Yeah, he probably is. I mean, anybody that can ride up the Alps like that hardly catching a breath, that is abnormal in my book. Is he mentally ill? Of course he is not mentally ill. Of course he is not mentally ill, and so we would not apply that to him. The statistical thing works to some extent.

Another standard is a moral standard. In fact, when I opened up my trench coat here, I was probably violating your moral standards, and you do not think it is appropriate. I am not likely to hurt you; in fact, exhibitionists—which is one of the one of the categories that we are going to talk about—statistically are not really very likely to harm you in any way. But people get very uncomfortable. It violates their standards somehow, and even though we could not show that they are statistically more likely to harm us, it still makes us uncomfortable. We really do not know what is coming next. So it bothers us.

Now those standards change over time. When I started teaching many years ago, I would lecture about the classifications of mental illness, and I would talk about homosexuality as a mental illness. And the American Psychiatric Association at that time classified it as a mental illness. It made people uncomfortable. It violated their moral standards, and they did not like homosexuality. That changed; and for the last, I think it is now, probably 30 years ago, that the American Psychiatric Association took homosexuality out of the classification system and said it is an alternative lifestyle it is okay. You are not mentally ill if you are a homosexual anymore. Well, why were people 50 years ago mentally ill and people are not now? Society's standards have changed. So from a moral point of view it has changed its basis. So that is another kind of classification, a way of a criterion that we can use to try to decide whether or not a person is abnormal.

Another one has to do with whether that person might harm us. In fact as we will see, for most states, harming somebody, including themselves, is one of the major criteria for locking somebody up in a mental institution. So maybe when I am banging my shoe on the wall over here, you do not care too much about that; if you can still hear me in the lecture why should you care. But in fact, you start thinking well if he is banging that shoe on the wall maybe next he is going to banging that shoe on me. So maybe I ought to be a little worried about this if he is this strange. I am not sure whether he is going to harm me or not. This is not helped by movies were people who are mentally ill are portrayed as characters with masks and knives and going around attacking people and that sort of thing.

For most classifications of mental illness, you are safer with that person than you are out in normal society. You go into a mental institution, in fact it is nowadays a pretty placid kind of place, and you are not likely to undergo harm at all in a place like that. But nevertheless, we fear that and we fear people hurting themselves or hurting us, and so that enters into our decision about whether or not to call something abnormal and whether or not that is mental illness.

Finally, we also, another criterion has to do with how unhappy the person is; how much they do not want to be the way they are. We do not always commit people to institutions. In many cases, people voluntarily go into institutions, and they do so because they are unhappy. They are not doing well and they want that somehow changed. And so that can be a criterion of mental illness too, if they are unhappy with their situation.

So all of these things have been used, and they are used sort of in a mixed way, and it is not always clear how we do this. We do the best that we can. It is a difficult process, because in many cases you have a continuum here of the behavior, and exactly where do you draw the line? Where do you make the mistake? Because, like any decision situation, you have people who are mentally ill and people who are not mentally ill, and these are overlapping distributions in terms of their behavior, and if you draw the line, you are going to make a mistake one way or the other. You are going to call somebody who is mentally ill, you are going to call them well; or you are going to call somebody who is well mentally ill. As you move that line back and forth you vary the proportion of errors, but you do not get rid of errors. So, sometimes it is a difficult decision to make. I have sat on and watched admission boards at hospitals where people sit around and argue about a particular diagnosis for somebody who has come into the mental institution. And they will not agree on those diagnoses. You say, how can they not agree on those things? Well, it is not always clear-cut. As we will see when we get into some of the classifications of mental illness, in fact, there are not hard and fast lines between these classifications.

Let us talk some about classifications and the history of classifications and the first question we might ask ourselves is, why would we want to classify somebody as having a mental illness or not? What is the advantage of being able to classify somebody? Well, according to the American Psychiatric Association—now you have to remember that psychiatrists are medical doctors; we talked about that in the first lecture. And the people who run the classification system—at least in this country—the people are members of the American Psychiatric Association, not the American Psychological Association. So they follow very strongly a medical kind of model, since they are medical doctors. What is the first thing you do when you go to the doctor's office? Well, the doctor comes out and diagnoses you. That means that the doctor is putting you into a classification system of some sort. And so the doctor may do various kinds of tests on you and try to decide where you fit. Do you have a stomachache or appendicitis? Those are two different classifications. And then the treatment is going to be dependent upon the classification.

And that would be nice, if we could follow the medical model in psychology and know exactly what the treatment is once we have made the diagnosis and classified somebody, but as I pointed out in a previous lecture, that does not always follow in psychology. Sometimes the therapy is more determined by the training of the therapist than by the particular diagnosis. The hope is that the diagnosis would tell you something about what therapies might be brought to bear to try to correct the condition.

So that is one reason to have a classification system, and probably the major reason for classifying mental illnesses. There are other reasons why you might want to do it. In fact, we are about to talk about some classification systems. And the real impetus for a classification system in this country came out of a clerical reason. After the Second World War, when people were being released from the military, they had to sort of classify what their condition was, and they often did not have a box to check to say what their mental condition was because we did not have a very good classification system at that point. So it was around 1952 that we got the first official classification system from the American Psychiatric Association, and that was partly driven by the necessity of this clerical task of sort of putting people into the box.

Today we have a clerical duty that is even greater than that, the insurance companies and the third-party payers for people with mental illnesses. They want to know what the classification of the person is. So, in fact, if you are a therapist and dealing with a particular patient, one of the first things you have to do is make a diagnosis and write down the number from the classification system that says what category this person fits into. Because then the insurance company says that you can do certain things, you can have a certain number of sessions of therapy if the person has this particular classification; but it is very different for this other classification. So again, it is kind of a clerical matter here.

Now there are some problems with classification systems. There are some problems, like self-fulfilling prophecies. Once you have classified somebody in a particular way, people expect you—the label tells them something about your behavior. There was a famous kind of study that was done where people voluntarily committed themselves to a mental institution; in fact to several different—I think there were eight different institutions that they committed themselves to. These were just sort of normal people who were committed to these institutions they self-committed themselves. They said okay I am not feeling well, I have these, I am hearing voices that are saying things like "dull" and "thud;" and they tried to use a category which was an existential psychosis, which is a category hardly anybody fit into. But they reported this upon entry into the institution.

Then the question was how likely was it that they were to get out and what would they be classified as when they did get out. In fact, after that, they stopped simulating any abnormal behavior; and they were in the institution on average, as I recall, it was over a month in the institution before they let them back out again. And without exception, they were classified as—because they were put in—most of them as schizophrenic; because they had been hearing voices, and that is one of the major indications of schizophrenia, they were classified as schizophrenia. Then when they were let out they were classified as schizophrenia in remission. They did not say they were normal again; they had been classified, and so now they could not get rid of that label. In fact, some of these people in the institutions would do such things as write down and take lots of notes, and they would look at their behavior and they would say "note-taking behavior," as if that is sort of a symptom of schizophrenia. Once they have the label, what they do is sort of tainted by the label, and so there can be kind of a self-fulfilling prophecy in classification, which is not a good thing.

Let us talk some then about classification systems and the history of these. They have been around for a long time. We know people have dealt with mental illness for a long time. In fact if you go into some of the archeological digs, they have dug up skulls of people who have little holes chipped in their head, a process called trephining, that they apparently did to release the bad spirits in the persons' heads. We do not know because no history has been written of this;

we can only infer what goes on from finding the skulls. But that is the idea, and in fact some of these people apparently lived. There are cases of the hole healing up, to some extent, so the person survived the operation, apparently; and maybe it did help them, because probably in some of these cases they had brain pressure from an accident and that may have relieved the brain pressure to some extent.

Mental illness has been around for a while, and we have had some therapy for mental illness. If you look about the first case of trying to classify this, Hippocrates—he lived from 460–377 B.C., so this was a long time ago—Hippocrates is considered the father of medicine. You may be familiar with the Hippocratic Oath that doctors take that is named after Hippocrates; he is the father of medicine. And as the father of medicine, it should not be surprising that he took the first crack at classifying mental illnesses. He classified into three categories: mania, melancholia, and a thing called phrenitis, which is a brain fever of some sort. I do not know much about phrenitis. Mania is probably what we called psychotic today; somebody who is sort of running around out of control. And melancholia is probably what we call depression today. So he had these three different classification systems, and he had certain theories about why this was, including bodily fluids and bile and other things that were happening. We are not going to get into any detail about that, but he had a whole theoretical system that supported this classification system.

Then in the Islamic tradition, Avicenna, from Arabia 980–1037, added a couple of classifications to it; he included epilepsy as one of them, and also included hysteria, which we talked about in the last lecture, in fact. We talked about psychoanalytic theory and how many of Freud's early patients were categorized as hysteria—which we now call conversion disorder—where you have part of the body that does not work quite properly and it has a psychological root cause to it. So, he added those two categories to it; and we are still talking here over 1,000 years ago that this classification system was being proposed.

Then not much happened after that for many, many hundreds of years. This is partly because people totally misunderstood mental illness. They thought that mental illness was caused by demons for the most part, and that was a religious experience. And so they—it was the era of witches and that kind of thing, instead of considering mental illness to be a medical condition—and if it is just demons, how do you classify a demon? A demon can do almost anything a demon wants to. So there wasn't much in the way of classification at that point.

Then in the 20th Century, we did start formal classification systems, and I already alluded to one of the reasons that we wanted a classification system in terms of the military being released from the Second World War. So the American Psychiatric Association decided that they would start an official classification system at that point. They used some of the classifications that had sort of been left over from history as a starting point. The other thing that they used was psychoanalytic theory that we just got through talking about, because psychoanalytic theory provided a theoretical context for many of these mental illnesses, which is part of the reason I wanted to talk about psychoanalytic theory before we talked about mental illnesses.

They came up with what is called the Diagnostic and Statistical Manual of Mental Disorders, commonly referred to as "DSM," the Diagnostic and Statistical Manual. The first one that came out we now call DSM-I, because there have been subsequent DSMs, and that came out in 1952. And then it took them about 15 years to come up with a new one, DMS-II. And then the times got shorter and shorter; and so I think we are coming out with a new official one about every seven or eight years now, and there is often a revision in the middle of that process too, DSM-II, DSM-III, DSM-III-R. We are now on DSM-IV, and were on DSM-TR, which is another revision called "Text Revision," that is what TR stands for. So we have sort of new versions of this kind of thing from time to time. Supposedly, as we learn more, we change this diagnostic and statistical manual, and gets thicker and thicker and the number of classifications become larger and larger. Over the years, this has changed in a number of ways. The original one, as I had mentioned, had a lot to do with the theoretical underpinnings of psychoanalysis and psychoanalytic theory. They got rid of that really between DSM-II and DSM-III. DSM-II, as I recall, had about seven different classifications in it. DSM-III had a whole bunch more classifications, because under DSM-II for example, you had neurosis as a category, and then were a number of different kinds of anxiety disorders under that, and it was all in kind of a psychoanalytic model.

Then they broke all of that out in DSM-III. And DSM-III tried very hard to become atheoretical and to get rid of this sort of underlying psychoanalytic structure that had propped up DSM-II. DSM-III also made quite a breakthrough in that they were far more concerned with specifying the exact sort of symptoms a person had to have. And now, in DSM-IV, in fact, we are down to the point where as I go through DSM-IV and we talk about some of these symptoms, we will get lists, like you have to have this or this, and you have to have three out of the following five things in order to be diagnosed with this particular disorder. So, it is very much more driven by observing the person and trying to decide whether—there is still some subjectivity to this; you cannot get rid of all of that, but because they have been able to do that, they have been able to make the system far more both reliable and valid. By reliable, we mean that if you have one person who is doing the diagnosis—take a particular case—that person gives a classification to it; how likely is it that a second clinician would give the same classification to it. If they do, then that is a fairly reliable system. And DMS-II was very unreliable; people disagreed quite a bit about these things. In fact, people disagreed with themselves. If you ask them at a particular time to diagnose a particular condition, and then ask them a year later, give them the same symptoms, people could not even agree with themselves necessarily on it because it was so nebulous, so ambiguous the descriptions of the classifications.

One thing that has been achieved with DSM-IV is much more reliability. Now validity, we are not quite so sure about, because you are never quite sure. How do you know for sure what the person has? Validity means that you have classified it correctly; that it indeed is the disorder you have just called it. We do know that if it is not reliable, it is not going to be very valid. That does not say whether it is the correct thing. They had a good list of diagnostic criteria for whether or not somebody was a witch a number of centuries ago. They were quite reliable about it, but were they valid? Well we do not think so today, because we do not think that there are witches today. So validity is a bit of a different concept, and we are not quite as sure about that, even with today's fairly sophisticated systems.

Let us look at DSM-IV–TR™ and see what it looks like in terms of how you diagnose mental illnesses. DSM-IV–TR™ actually has five axes, so there are five diagnoses that enter into the final description of what the person has. The first axis is usually considered to be the most important, because that is the clinical diagnosis that the person has. That would say that the person is bipolar, or that the person is schizophrenic, or the person has depression or anxiety disorder or something like that. That would be on the first axis. So most of what we are going to talk about in here is going to be on Axis I; it is the clinical condition that the person has, a clinical syndrome. A syndrome is a collection of symptoms that a person would have.

Axis II contains personality disorders and also mental retardation. So a person might have a particular clinical symptom—suppose that the person has schizophrenia—but that person may also have a personality disorder. Perhaps this person is a paranoid personality as well as perhaps being a schizophrenic, and so they would get both of these diagnoses, one of Axis I and one on Axis II. Or the person may have some form of mental retardation as well as having a clinical condition of some sort. So they would get a diagnosis on each of those axes in that case.

Axis III has to do with the medical condition of the person, so the person might have a particular mental disorder, might have a personality disorder, and might be diabetic on top of that, or have chronic pain or something like that. That would be a medical diagnosis on Axis III.

Axis IV evaluates the psychosocial or environmental stressors that might be present. So they might have a clinical condition, might have a personality disorder, might have diabetes, and they are also living in a high stress household where the father has been missing and the mother has ten kids and there is a lot of yelling and screaming; and that would be a diagnosis there.

The fifth axis is a global assessment of how the person is functioning at the current time. So you would say, how is this person doing? This person cannot communicate; this person is mute, for example. So that would be an indication of that person's functioning at this particular time.

This particular system would give a person really five diagnoses, and that would be all part of the pattern, and each of those things might say something different about what kind of treatment the person should get.

Let us just look finally here at the various prevalence of major disorders—and we will talk in much more detail about these major disorders—but let us look just very briefly about, over a 12-month period of time, how likely would it be that somebody you would find would have a particular disorder? The first figure I have is that mental illness affects 37 million adults in the country during a given year, and that is about 18.5% of the population. So, if you are walking down the street and people are passing you on the street, you know that about one in five of those people are having a mental problem of some sort. Now, it might not be debilitating; this person is not going to jump out and kill you, but this person may be depressed, may have anxiety about certain things. So about one in five have some form of a disorder. Anxiety disorders affect nearly 12% of the population in any given particular year, and those include things like panic disorders, phobias, and we will talk about those as we go along. Mood disorders such as depression and bipolar disorder affect a little over 5% of the population; depression—unipolar depression being the major one of those—so that is about 5% of the population. Substance-abuse disorders including alcohol and drugs affect about 6% of the population in any one year—now the rate of alcoholism itself is higher than that over a lifetime—but in any particular year. And schizophrenia affects about 1% of the population. You might say, why do we spend so much time talking about schizophrenia if it is only 1% of the population? Well, it is such a severe disorder, that schizophrenia accounts for so many of the hospital beds in mental institutions, and so much of the time and effort is spent on mental patients, that it is a major disorder even though it does not affect that many people.

So we are going to go through these classifications in the next series of lectures and talk about the various mental disorders, the various symptoms that occur with these. We are going to have just a preliminary—I asked the question, what might be causing these kinds of thing? And go right through the Diagnostic and Statistical Manual, and try to learn it at least at the level that we would be able to recognize mental illness when we see it.

So today we have talked a little bit about why people are considered abnormal: what criteria are used, some statistical criteria, moral criteria, whether or not they are likely to harm us, whether or not they are happy with their condition. And we have also talked historically about some of the classification systems and what today's modern classification system looks like and what the axes are on that system. From here on out we are going to be talking in much more detail about the individual classifications. Thank you.

Lecture Eight
Anxiety and Mood Disorders

Scope:

Two of the major classifications of mental illness are anxiety and mood disorders. The former, which was earlier called *neurosis*, has as its major symptom a feeling of apprehension about possible danger. *Phobias* are undue fears of specific objects or situations, including fears of animals, natural environments, blood-injection-injury, and situations. Phobias are more prevalent in women and are treated with behavior therapies. *Panic disorders* involve activation of fight-or-flight responses with no appropriate stimulus. These occur and subside quickly and can lead to agoraphobia, fear of crowds. They are treated with both cognitive-behavioral therapies and drugs. *Generalized anxiety disorder* involves long-term worry about many life domains, with such symptoms as unhappiness or tension. Treatments include tranquilizers and cognitive-behavioral therapies. Mood disorders include *unipolar and bipolar depression*. Unipolar depression affects more women than men and includes the milder *dysthymia* and major depressive disorder, both of which are classified by the number and duration of symptoms. Treatments for depression include drugs, psychotherapies, and electroconvulsive therapy. Bipolar disorders include both depressive and manic episodes; the latter involves euphoric moods that are sometimes so severe that behavior becomes psychotic. Treatments for depressive phases are similar to those for unipolar depression and, for manic phases, include lithium and anticonvulsive and antipsychotic drugs.

Outline

I. *Anxiety disorders* are also sometimes called *neuroses* and have as a symptom a feeling of apprehension about possible danger.

   A. A *phobia* is an undue fear of a specific object or situation that may cause avoidant behavior.

      1. Animal subtype phobias include undue fear of snakes, spiders, dogs, and other animals.

      2. Natural environment subtype includes fear of heights and water.

3. Blood-injection-injury subtype includes fear of hypodermic needles and the sight of blood.

4. Situational subtype includes fear of particular situations, such as flying in an airplane or riding in an elevator.

5. Atypical subtype includes fear of events that are difficult to classify, such as choking or vomiting.

6. The prevalence of phobias is about 16% for women and 7% for men.

7. Phobias can often be treated with behavior therapies, as will be discussed in a future lecture.

B. *Panic disorders* involve the unexpected activation of the fight-or-flight response of the sympathetic nervous system with no apparent appropriate stimulus.

1. A panic attack is often misidentified by the person experiencing it as a medical problem, such as a heart attack.

2. Panic attacks are distinguished from generalized anxiety by how quickly they develop (10 minutes) and subside (30 minutes).

3. Panic attacks sometimes lead to agoraphobia, the fear of crowds and public places.

4. The prevalence of panic disorders is about 5% for women and 2% for men.

5. Treatments for panic disorders include both cognitive-behavioral treatments and medications, such as minor tranquilizers and antidepressants.

C. *Generalized anxiety disorder* is characterized by chronic, excessive worry about life events.

1. In this case, the apprehension is not toward a specific situation or event but includes many concerns, such as work, money, relationships, and so on.

2. Symptoms include unhappiness, difficulty concentrating, tension, headaches, and sleep disturbances.

3. Treatments for generalized anxiety disorder include medications, such as minor tranquilizers, and cognitive-behavioral therapies.

D. *Obsessive-compulsive disorder* (OCD) is characterized by both intrusive, recurring thoughts and repetitive behaviors.

    1. Obsessions are thoughts that are recurring, disturbing, and inappropriate.

    2. Compulsions are difficult-to-resist behaviors that are usually highly repetitive.

    3. Of those with OCD, up to 67% also are depressed.

    4. Treatments for OCD include behavioral therapies and antidepressant drugs (especially selective serotonin reuptake inhibitors).

II. The two most common types of mood disorder are *unipolar depression* and *bipolar depression.*

    A. Normal depressions that result from recent stress, such as the loss of a loved one, are not mood disorders.

        1. Lifetime prevalence rates for unipolar depression are 13% in males and 21% in females.

        2. The milder form of unipolar depression is called *dysthymia* and requires a person to have a depressed mood for most of the day, for more days than not, for at least 2 years and to have at least two of the following symptoms: appetite change, sleep disturbance, low energy, low self-esteem, concentration problems, and feelings of hopelessness.

        3. Those with major depressive disorder must experience either depressed mood or loss of interest in pleasurable activities and three or four of the following (for a total of five symptoms): fatigue, sleep disturbance, appetite change, slowdown of activity, concentration difficulty, self-denunciation, and recurrent thoughts of death or suicide.

        4. There is a recurrence of major depression in about 80% of cases.

        5. Treatments for unipolar depression include antidepressant drugs (tricyclic and serotonin reuptake inhibitors), psychotherapies, and for severely depressed or drug-resistant patients, electroconvulsive therapy (ECT).

B. Bipolar disorders include both depressive episodes and manic episodes; the latter are characterized by markedly elevated or euphoric mood.

1. Lifetime risk for bipolar disorder is about 1%, with no sex differences.

2. The depressive episodes are largely indistinguishable from unipolar depression.

3. The manic phases may be so severe that patients become psychotic and have a break with reality.

4. Many of history's most creative people apparently had bipolar disorder and were most productive in the hypomanic phase, (for example, Robert Schumann and Virginia Woolf).

5. Treatments for the depressive phase are similar to those for unipolar depression; for manic episodes, lithium and anticonvulsive drugs are used for mood stabilization and antipsychotic drugs for psychotic symptoms.

C. A major risk with depressive disorders is suicide.

1. In the United States, suicide attempts are three to four times more likely in women than men, while completion rates are three to four times higher in men.

2. The highest rate of completed suicides is for those 65 years of age or older.

3. Among those who commit suicide, most have recently talked to family or friends about suicide or about death or dying, but only about 50% have seen a professional.

Essential Reading:

James Butcher, Susan Mineka, and Jill Hooley, *Abnormal Psychology*, 12th ed., chapters 6 and 7.

Supplementary Reading:

American Psychiatric Association, *Diagnostic and Statistical Manual of Mental Disorders*, 4th ed.

Kay Redfield Jamison, *Touched with Fire: Manic-Depressive Illness and the Artistic Temperament.*

Questions to Consider:

1. Do you think that depression has any useful function in human life?

2. Do you think that bipolar disorder is just an extreme version of the normal mood swings we all go through, or do you think it is an entirely separate condition?

Lecture Eight—Transcript
Anxiety and Mood Disorders

We have now talked about classification systems for mental illness and talked a little bit about what makes abnormal behavior abnormal, and I promised you last time that we were going to start to go through DSM-IV and look at some of the classifications of mental disorders. And so we are going to start that process in this lecture.

Today we are going to look at two of the major classifications of mental illness, anxiety and mood disorders. If you will recall, in the last lecture, I mentioned the prevalence, the one-year prevalence of various disorders, and for anxiety disorder it was 12%, and for mood disorder it was about 5%, and those are very high. So what we are talking about today comprises an awful lot of what you see as mental health problems out there. Now as we will see, many of these health problems are not such that a person would be institutionalized for them. In many cases, they are just unhappy, and it might affect their job to some extent and their ability to socialize and some other kinds of things, although they would not necessarily be institutionalized. Nevertheless, they are very important kinds of problems. So we are going to go over anxiety disorders and the sub-classification of anxiety disorders including phobias and panic disorders; also generalized anxiety disorder and obsessive-compulsive disorders. So those are some of the sub-classifications under anxiety disorders.

Then under mood disorders, we are going to talk about the two major classifications, unipolar mood disorder or depression, and bipolar depression as well. And finally we are going to talk a little about suicide at the end as well.

So let us talk some about anxiety. Anxiety as a classification has been around for a long time. We use to call it neurosis, and when I talked about Freud you may remember that I mentioned neurosis and the fact that he was dealing with neurotic patients—for the most part people with hysteria, which is an anxiety disorder. Between DSM-II and DSM-III, we started calling them anxiety disorders, so these have been around for quite a while. And, in general, anxiety is about what you would think it would be. It is an apprehension about a possible danger; and that apprehension might be a more generalized apprehension that we will talk about in a minute, or it might be fairly specific, for example phobias. Phobias are undue fears about specific objects or situations that a person might get into, and these cause avoidant behavior. So once they have the phobia, they then avoid the behavior. And when we talk later, in learning theory, a little bit about avoidance learning, we will discover that this may be a cycle where they get the fear, they avoid it, and that in fact reinforces the fear again. So phobias are sometimes difficult to get rid of once we get them.

So we have this undue fear of specific objects. And then there are some sub-classifications under phobia. For example, animal phobias include the fear of snakes, spiders, dogs, and other kinds of animals. Now that might not be surprising to you, and it should not surprise you really at all, because of the evolutionary psychologists who have looked at phobias in a universal—in a universal, across cultures—a fear of spiders and snakes. Everybody is afraid of spiders and snakes. So, in some respects, perhaps we are all mentally ill in some ways, but most of us do not let it affect our behavior; we do not refuse to go out in our backyard because we are afraid a snake might get us. But we have that fear, and it is probably built in to us; there is probably an adaptation. Our ancestors tended to survive if they were afraid of snakes and spiders, and those that were not afraid of it tended not to have offspring. So this is probably a built-in adaptation that generally works pretty well, but in fact, if it is too strong, it can lead to some debilitating kinds of behaviors. "Natural environments" subtype includes fear of heights and water, and perhaps some other things like earthquakes and tornados and that sort of thing as well. And again there might be some adaptive value to that, but it can be overdone.

A third type is blood injection, or injury subtype, in which you can have fear of hypodermic needles and the sight of blood. I know, for example, one of my sons is particularly fearful of hypodermic needs. I hope he grows out of it as he has more experience with those kinds of things. Situational subtype includes particular situations, such as flying an airplane, being afraid of that; or riding in an elevator. Then an atypical subtype would include things like having fear of choking or vomiting, something like that.

So these are all phobias. They are fairly prevalent in the population, and more prevalent in women than in more. About 16% of women have phobias, and about 7% of men have phobias; so it is more prevalent in women. Phobias, once you get them, are fairly easily dealt with with behavior therapies, and we will talk about that when we talk about therapies and how you would do this. It is a learning therapy, where you have a person relearn an appropriate response to this undue fear of a particular stimulus, and that can be usually fairly successfully done.

Panic disorders are a second kind of anxiety disorder. With panic disorders, there is not a particular stimulus that sets it off so much. Panic disorders; somebody might be out, let us say shopping or something like that, and driving home in her car and suddenly her heart starts to race, she starts to breathe very shallowly, she breaks out in a cold sweat, she thinks she is having a heart attack. And she might get out of the car and start running along the sidewalk, trying to get somebody to help her because she thinks she is having this medical problem and it is a very severe kind of thing. That would be a description of a panic attack that somebody might have. These are distinguished from generalized anxiety disorders that we are about to talk about by how quickly they come on—they develop in 10 minutes or less in general—and how quickly they subside. They usually go away in about 30 minutes or so, so if you run across somebody having this, if you could just quiet them down for a while, generally it will go away. There are people who do think that they are having a medical problem when this happens, and people go to the hospital with these panic attacks—at least early on—when they think that is what their problem is.

In some cases panic attacks can lead to agoraphobia. Agoraphobia is a fear of crowds or a fear of public places, and that may be combined with a panic attack of some sort. And people with agoraphobia, sometimes if it is severe enough, end up being home ridden. They stay home. They order out their groceries, they do not leave their— they do not cross their front door for months at a time, if they have a severe form of agoraphobia.

The prevalence of panic disorders is about 5% for women and about 2% for men, although that is probably an underestimate. I am not sure we know all of the people who have this. In fact, they have gone into a college population of women, and in that population, 30 or 40% of the women will claim that they have had an incident like this in the previous year, but not severe enough that they would go to a doctor about it and be diagnosed for it. So, we are probably underestimating the prevalence of panic attacks.

Panic attacks can be dealt with through cognitive-behavioral therapy, to some extent like phobias, as I mentioned a minute ago. And also medications, such as minor tranquilizers and anti-depressants, can be effective with panic attacks as well.

Generalized anxiety disorder is another sub-classification of anxiety disorder. And with generalized anxiety disorder, you have a chronic excessive worry about life events. So there is not a specific precipitating stimulus that kicks it off, nor is it like a panic attack that sort of comes on quickly and then goes away; but in fact it is a chronic kind of condition where you just feel like things are not right. The symptoms include unhappiness, difficulty concentrating, tension, headaches, sleep disturbances, and that sort of thing, and it affects much of life.

I play a tape often for my students of somebody with a generalized anxiety disorder, and this is a young lady—I believe she is 17 years old—and she is living in a house which is not a desirable place to live. Her father is sometimes indicating he might sexually molest her, and he is pretty tough on the kids, spanks them and throws them around a little bit. So it is not a nice situation, and you might say her problem is due to that situation. But, in fact, when you talk to her about this problem, she says she is afraid of everything. She is afraid of the mother some of the time. She barricades her door to keep people out of it, and stuffs a towel into the door locks so nobody can look in, and sometimes sleeps with a knife and has dreams of people coming attacking her at night. She says she is just afraid of everything; and that is sort of a characteristic of generalized anxiety disorder.

The final subcategory of anxiety disorder is obsessive-compulsive disorder, sometimes called OCD. Obsessive-compulsive disorder is really the combination of a couple of disorders here. These are intrusive recurring thoughts and repetitive behaviors. So the thought part is the obsession. Somebody has an obsession; it means that they have recurring, disturbing, and inappropriate kinds of thoughts about things. So perhaps somebody sits and thinks a lot about how they do not want to have germs around them and they want everything to be clean, and they are afraid that somebody is going to come through the door that has disease and they might get this disease. Somebody like Howard Hughes, for example, was obsessive-compulsive with this particular disorder, where he was afraid that he was going to get infected with something. So he thinks about this and it takes over his thoughts. We all have some kind of obsessive thoughts. I sometimes carry music around in my head—where I sing in a choir and I will get a piece of music going—and for half a week, this will pop up from time to time as kind of an obsessive thought. It does not bother me very much that this is the case. It does not seem to affect my behavior otherwise. But if you have that kind of thing, you can understand a little bit about what these people are going through when they have these kinds of obsessive thoughts.

These then lead to compulsive behaviors. The behavior part is the compulsions, where they then do not do certain kinds of things; they do not step on the crack—you will step on the crack, break your mother's back kind of thing, where people walk down the sidewalk and never step on the crack; or people, particularly if they have these obsessive thoughts about diseases, they may repetitively wash their hands. Somebody may wash his or her hands eight times or something like that. There is a woman that I am familiar with who is a nurse and afraid of HIV, and its become an obsessive kind of thing with her where she thinks about it all the time, that she might get HIV, and so she goes home and washes her hands and will not let her kids touch her because she is afraid they will get HIV and that sort of thing. So that is the compulsive part of this obsessive-compulsive disorder. OCD, of those who have obsessive-compulsive disorder, about 67% about two-thirds are also are depressed. So we have what is called co-morbidity, where they have more than really one condition that is leading to their behavior.

Treatments for obsessive-compulsive disorder, there are behavioral therapies, so that is where they try to treat it with that; and also antidepressant drugs, especially the selective serotonin re-uptake inhibitors like Prozac, are used for people with this disorder, and have been found to have some benefit for people with that disorder.

Moving on then to mood disorders. As I have mentioned at the beginning of this lecture, there are two major sub-classifications of mood disorders; these are unipolar depression and bipolar depression. Now whether or not these are the same disorder in terms of being just a different version of the same disorder, we are not quite sure. It looks like it is probably unlikely that is the case. For example, I will cite it in a minute with depressive disorders, unipolar depression, women are far more likely to have this than men. For the case of bipolar disorder, it is about an equal distribution of women and men, which indicates that there might be a difference in this. If you look at inheritability of the disorders, there is also a difference for depression and for bipolar disorder.

Now we are not here talking about normal depression. Everybody has depressions. If you had a loved one that dies, people become depressed; and this may go on for three months or so, which would be considered a normal kind of depressed period for having lost somebody. So that is not what we are talking about here. We are talking about depression where there does not seem to be a major precipitating event, and which seems to come over somebody and they are unable to shake it, even with time.

Unipolar depression, the prevalence rates for the lifetime—not the one year rate, but for a lifetime—are 13% in males and 21% in females, so women are more likely to have unipolar depression, or be what is sometimes called clinical depressed. The milder form of unipolar depression is called dysthymia, and it requires—according to the classification system—the person to have a depressed mood for most of the day, for more days than not, for at least two years—but it is considerably milder than unipolar depression—and also to have at least two of the following symptoms: appetite change, sleep disturbance, low energy, low self-esteem, concentration problems, and feelings of hopelessness. So those are all symptoms of this dysthymia, which is sort of milder form of unipolar depression.

Those with major depressive disorders experience—and this is one of the cases where we have sort of a menu of things that a person could have—this person must experience either a depressed mood or a loss of interest in pleasurable activities; one of those two is required. But it is interesting, isn't it, that depressed mood is not required? You can actually have depression without necessarily being overly sad or having a depressed mood. If you have the set of symptoms that we are about to read off here, you can be depressed and be diagnosed as clinically depressed, even though overwhelming sadness is not one of the symptoms.

And so people are often not appropriately diagnosed with it. In fact, it is estimated that only about half the people who have depression are ever diagnosed with depression, and many of those have been to many doctors before they get a proper diagnosis for depression, because it is a bit elusive and sometimes you do not have to have major sadness. So you have to have one of those two things that I mentioned: either a depressed mood or a loss of interest in pleasurable activities; and then you have to have three or four of the following—so you have to have a total of five symptoms: fatigue, sleep disturbance, appetite change, slowdown of activity, concentration difficulty, self-denunciation, recurrent thoughts of death or suicide. So if you have an appropriate number of those, then you would fit the criteria for a diagnosis of unipolar depression.

There is a recurrence of major depression in about 80% of the cases; and the more often you have depression, the more you have a recurrence, the more likely it is that you will have an additional recurrence as well. So you get people who have depression, and they start an anti-depressive drug and they are starting to feel pretty good, and they quit taking the drug, even though their doctor told them to continue taking the drug. It is quite likely that person will have a recurrence of depression if they quit taking the drug.

Treatments for unipolar depression include antidepressant drugs; and there are several versions of those. There are tricyclic drugs, which are the more old-fashioned of the drugs for combating depression, and they have some side effects that are not too desirable; and serotonin re-uptake inhibitors, like Prozac and Wellbutrin and some of the other kinds of drugs that are available now for depression. And we will talk in more detail about those drugs later, and in particular about some of the recent concerns that people have, particularly with adolescents taking these drugs and the possibility of suicide. Psychotherapies are also sometimes used for depression. And for severely depressed people—especially drug resistant patients— where you have tried about everything that you can with them, sometimes electroconvulsive shock therapy, or ECT, is used for severely depressed people. And we will talk in some detail when we get into therapies about ECT and its effectiveness. It turns out that, for those people, ECT works pretty well, and there is some hope for these folks even if they are resistant to drug therapies.

Bipolar disorders are another of the sub-categories of the mood disorders. And bipolar disorders are very interesting, because they have, not only the depressive episodes that you expect with unipolar depression, but they also have manic episodes as well; and there is a swing between the depressed episode and the manic episode, and it is not quite sure how long even this swing should be. In the more typical cases, the swing is on the order of weeks or even months, but there are rapidly cycling people who are bipolar as well, where these swings may be a bit faster than that.

Now this is one point in the course where sometimes I have people coming up to me after I lecture and saying, I think I have it. I have these mood swings all the time, some days I am just really up and some days I am really down. And I try to assure them that it is probably not the case that they have it. We all have mood swings, and some days we are up and some days we are down. We are talking about very severe mood swings when we talk about bipolar disorders. These mood swings, I will describe some here in a minute. The lifetime risk for bipolar disorder is about 1%, and this one, as I mentioned a minute ago, does not have sex differences, where unipolar depression does have sex differences. The depressive episodes are largely indistinguishable from unipolar depression; and in fact the person may have unipolar depression for some period of time and then later swing into the manic kind of phases as well. So the original diagnosis is often unipolar depression, before the manic phase kicks in. The manic phases have different amounts of severity to them. In some cases, these can be very severe and can lead to even psychotic behavior, in which case anti-psychotic drugs may even be prescribed for these. Psychotic behavior—we have not used that term before—that is basically where there is a break from reality, and the person becomes sort of detached from the world, even in knowing who they are or where they are; and so it is a very sever form of mental illness.

I had a neighbor once who became manic-depressive. And this fellow, at a certain point he suddenly had a Harley Davidson motorcycle sitting in his garage. Then he went out and bought a new car. He bought some real estate on the coast. And he would just talk about these things and be going and seemed as happy as could be about it. The police followed him one day, he had been speeding down the highway, did not know quite what he was doing, and it turned out he had bipolar disorder and was entering a manic phase in that disorder.

We had a graduate student in my program, and this poor young lady was fairly new in the program, and was working with a fellow who had a laboratory that had some animals in it. She was a teaching assistant and she was supposed to come in and take care of the animals on the weekend. She came in this one time and could not get into the laboratory because she forgot her key, so she found something to knock the door down, and picked up a piece of furniture and slammed in the door enough times, it knocked the door down. Then she fed the animals, and then she could not figure out how to lock the door back up. So she went to the hardware store and bought herself a big chain and a lock and locked the door shut with this chain so that her adviser could not even get into his own laboratory anymore.

It turned out that she was doing other bizarre kinds of things. She bought a new car as well. She went out, she would sell cosmetics and other kinds of things—flea market kinds of things. She set up her stand to sell these things, a table next to a four-lane highway, where people could not even pull off the side of the highway; trying to sell these things with no recognition that this was a totally inappropriate thing to do. Her judgment was completely impaired. She did unusual and bizarre kinds of things, and finally her husband recognized this enough, as did the rest of us, and we got her some help. And she ended up, in fact, being institutionalized for a period of time until they got her medication straightened out where this was not a problem.

That is an example of sort of the extreme case of the manic phase. Now the manic phase is not always hypermanic (that would be hypermanic, what I was just describing). The manic phase can be hypomanic as well, meaning a little less than manic. People who are hypomanic are actually very pleasant to be around and they enjoy themselves a lot. It used to be that, in mental institutions, if you want to find somebody to sort of produce a talent show or something like that, find a hypomanic person who is in the hypomanic phase of being bipolar, and as long as they can hold it in the hypomanic phase, they will be terrific at it. They do not sleep much; they are awake, kind of like they are on amphetamines or something like that. They are quite productive before they cross over the boundary into the hypermanic phase where they no longer can use good judgment. In fact, many people who are quite creative have been diagnosed as bipolar. Some we know are bipolar, people like Hemmingway, for example. And some people we kind of infer that they are bipolar because they lived a long time ago before these classifications even came along; but just a partial list of people: Lord Byron, Herman Melville, Edgar Allen Poe, Rossetti, Shelley, Tennyson; and then others like Balzac, Virginia Woolf, F. Scott Fitzgerald, Charles Lamb; I already mentioned Ernest Hemmingway; among composers, people like Handel, Schumann, Mahler, Rossini, Tchaikovsky, Rachmaninoff. All of these people, it has been—there is fair evidence that these people were bipolar.

One of the problems with trying to correct bipolar disorder is that people who are bipolar often like being bipolar. They really do not want to change, because this hypomanic phase is so much fun to be in. They feel so creative and so fulfilled when they are in this phase. If you get then on proper medication it sort of flattens out their affect, and they do not have these highs that they can have where they have these bursts of creativity that allow them to do the kinds of things that this list of people did in life. In fact, from an evolutionary point of view, being plagued bipolar is perhaps a good adaptation, at least if you can keep it in the hypomanic phase, because these people can really be quite creative and move societies along quite nicely.

So at any rate, bipolar disorder, one of the real problems is people often go off the medication because they do not like what it does to them. It changes them into a different person, they think, and so that is one of the problems with this. But if you can do it, treatments for the depressive phase are usually antidepressive treatments like Prozac and the other drugs, and then for the manic phase are things like lithium that is been used for at least half a century now against bipolar disorder. And then, more recently, anticonvulsive drugs have been found to be effective against the manic phase of bipolar as well. And if the manic phase goes hypermanic into psychotic episodes, then sometimes the antipsychotic drugs are used as well; and we will talk about the antipsychotic drugs later in the course.

One of the problems with depression and mood disorders is suicide; people are more likely to commit suicide. In the U.S., suicide attempts for women are about three to four times more likely than for men. But, on the other hand, men are three or four times more likely to commit suicide than women; to be successful at committing suicide. It is a real problem. Suicide is often very much comorbid with other kinds of diagnoses as well, and one of the real things that lead you to want to get help for somebody—either unipolar depression or bipolar depression—is if their suicide ideation, if they are thinking about suicide, if they are thinking about death. In fact, if you look at people who do commit suicide, most of them have recently talked to their family about suicide or about death and dying; but only about half of them have ever gone to a therapist about this. So the best thing you can do if you hear somebody talking about this is try to get them to a therapist of some sort to try to get some help for the problem. It might surprise you to know that suicide rates that we often hear about with young people—and I work in a college setting and often we are worried that if one person commits suicide it would lead to a chain reaction of suicides, and that is a worry—but, in actual fact, suicide, completed suicides, are most prominent for people 65 years of age or older. Those people actually commit suicide more frequently than even the younger population does. So, it is important to recognize the possibility of suicide with depressed folks.

So today we have talked about two of the major classifications of mental disorders; talked about anxiety disorders and the sub-classifications of anxiety disorders, including the phobias, undue fear of object or situations, panic disorders. We have talked about generalized anxiety disorder, which is more pervasive and chronic. We talked about obsessive-compulsive disorders, the problems with obsessive thoughts and compulsive behaviors. Then we talked about mood disorders and the two major sub-classifications of that: unipolar depression and also bipolar depression. So these are very important categories, and ones we should be aware of as we are talking about mental illness. Thank you.

Lecture Nine
Disorders of Brain, Body, Self, Drugs, Sex

Scope:

Cognitive disorders result from brain impairments that lead to disturbances of consciousness or deficits in cognition or memory. Alzheimer's disease is the most frequent cause, although stroke, Parkinson's disease, and injury are also possible causes. Somatoform disorders involve bodily complaints with no organic bases and include hypochondriasis, with complaints of one disease; somatization disorder, with complaints about multiple diseases; pain disorders; conversion disorders, which involve sensory or motor deficits; and body dysmorphic disorders, with perceived appearance flaws. Dissociative disorders include loss of self, called *depersonalization*; loss of memory, called *amnesia*; fugue, involving flight; and dissociative identity disorder, formerly called *multiple personalities*. Substance-related disorders involve physiological impairments due to substance abuse and the abuse itself. Sexual disorders involve dysfunctions, in which the disorder disturbs normal sexual functioning, and paraphilias, which involve a person receiving abnormal sexual gratification from objects, situations, or activities.

Outline

I. *Cognitive disorders* are the result of impairment of the brain.

    A. Brain impairments can be of three types.

        1. *Delirium* is characterized by a disturbance of consciousness that leads to confusion and disorientation; its most frequent cause is drug intoxication or withdrawal, particularly in the elderly.

        2. *Dementia* is characterized by multiple cognitive deficits and usually involves impairment of memory.

        3. *Amnestic disorders* are deficits in memory, usually without other cognitive impairments.

    B. The most frequently occurring type of dementia is the result of Alzheimer's disease (56% of dementia cases).

        1. Alzheimer's disease (AD) causes a slow but progressively deteriorating condition leading to death.

2. Although AD is increasingly likely with advancing age, early-onset AD may affect people in their 40s and 50s; early-onset AD is probably hereditary.

3. There are currently about 4 million people in the United States with AD, but this number is expected to triple in the next 50 years.

4. People with AD have protein plaques form on their brains that cause changes at both the neuronal level and the gross anatomical level.

5. There are currently no effective treatments for AD, although environmental interventions can improve quality of life.

C. Other major causes of dementia are stroke, Parkinson's disease, and brain injury.

D. The most frequently occurring cause of amnestic syndrome, which impairs memory, is chronic alcohol use.

II. *Soma* means body; thus, *somatoform disorders* involve conditions in which there are complaints about bodily symptoms or defects, but there are no corresponding organic bases.

A. With *hypochondriasis*, a person believes that he or she has a particular disease and the symptoms associated with that disease when physical exams fail to show medical abnormalities.

1. Those with hypochondriasis often are preoccupied by bodily functions, and this preoccupation persists for long periods of time (a minimum of 6 months).

2. Cognitive behavioral therapies show some benefit for this disorder.

B. *Somatization disorder* is similar to hypochondriasis but involves multiple physical complaints, including at a minimum, four pain symptoms, two gastrointestinal symptoms, one sexual symptom, and one pseudoneurological symptom.

C. *Pain disorders* involve persistent and severe pain in some area or areas of the body for which no medical condition can be found.

D. *Conversion disorder* is characterized by symptoms and deficits in sensory or motor functions of the body that cannot be explained by a medical condition, for example, partial paralysis or deafness.

E. A person with *body dysmorphic disorder* believes that he or she has a major bodily flaw that negatively affects his or her appearance to the extent that the person cannot function normally in social or work settings.

III. With *dissociative disorders*, some part of the normally well-integrated self becomes dissociated, or separated, from the other parts.

A. *Depersonalization* occurs when the sense of self is temporarily lost and the person feels that he or she does not really exist or is detached from reality.

B. *Dissociative amnesia* occurs when there is a memory loss, usually about the events in one's life or one's identity, for a period of time, but there is no physical precipitating condition.

C. *Fugue* means flight. With *dissociative fugue*, the person takes flight from his or her current life, begins a new life in a new location, and has amnesia of the previous life.

D. *Dissociative identity disorder*, formerly called *multiple personality disorder* or, more colloquially, *split personality*, is characterized by the person taking on two or more distinct identities.

    1. Note that this disorder is entirely separate from schizophrenia.

    2. The alter identities usually have no knowledge of the other identities, and switches between identities usually occur within seconds.

    3. Only 200 cases of dissociative identity disorder could be found prior to 1979, whereas in 1999, more than 30,000 cases had been reported.

    4. Part of the increased incidence may be due to the highly controversial possibility that some therapists are promoting the disorder, particularly for women who believe they have suffered childhood abuse.

IV. *Substance-related disorders* may include problems that occur as a result of taking a drug of abuse, the side effects of medication, or toxin exposure. (Most of the details of the first and largest category, drugs of abuse, will be discussed in a future lecture.)

A. One subcategory includes actual physiological impairments that are the result of prolonged and excessive ingestion of psychoactive drugs, such as alcohol abuse disorder (Korsakoff's syndrome).

B. The second major category includes addictive disorders resulting from the use of a substance.

    1. *Substance abuse* involves the pathological use of a substance that results in hazardous behavior or the continued use of the substance even in the face of negative consequences.

    2. *Substance dependence* is the physiological need for a substance to the point that tolerance develops and withdrawal symptoms can occur.

V. Sexual and gender-identity disorders group into three general categories that include *sexual dysfunctions*, *paraphilias*, and *gender-identity disorders*.

A. Someone who has a sexual dysfunction has a disturbance in sexual desire and the corresponding physiological reactions to the point that distress and interpersonal difficulty occur.

    1. Included in sexual dysfunctions are dysfunctions of sexual desire, such as hyposexual desire, in which there is little interest in sex, and sexual aversion disorder, in which sexual contact is avoided.

    2. Dysfunctions of sexual arousal include male erectile disorder (formerly *impotence*) and female sexual arousal disorder (formerly *frigidity*).

    3. Dysfunctions of orgasm include premature ejaculation in men and inability to achieve orgasm in both sexes.

    4. Sexual pain disorders occur when intercourse results in pain.

B. Paraphilias are characterized by frequent sexual urges, fantasies, or behaviors that involve unusual objects, activities, or situations and cause distress.

    1. Note that homosexuality was once listed under this category; it was voted off the list in 1973 and is no longer considered a mental disorder but a normal alternative lifestyle.

2. Fetishism involves a person receiving sexual gratification from the use of an inanimate object, such as an article of clothing, or a body part not normally considered sexually arousing.
3. Transvestic fetishism involves a man receiving sexual gratification by dressing in women's clothing.
4. Voyeurism, which is commonly called peeping, occurs when a man receives sexual gratification by observing unsuspecting women in a state of undress or engaged in sexual activity.
5. Exhibitionism (indecent exposure or flashing) involves exposing one's genitals to others inappropriately and without consent.
6. Sadism involves receiving sexual pleasure by inflicting pain on someone else.
7. Sexual masochism involves deriving sexual pleasure from receiving pain.
8. Frotteurism involves deriving sexual pleasure from touching or rubbing against someone without his or her consent.
9. Pedophilia involves sexual activity with a child.
10. There is also a catchall category for less frequently occurring paraphilias, such as sexual activities with corpses or animals.

C. Gender-identity disorder occurs when one has a strong cross-gender identification and a persistent discomfort with one's assigned sex.

Essential Reading:

James Butcher, Susan Mineka, and Jill Hooley, *Abnormal Psychology*, 12th ed., chapters 15, 8, 12, and 13.

Supplementary Reading:

American Psychiatric Association, *Diagnostic and Statistical Manual of Mental Disorders*, 4th ed.

S. O. Lilienfeld, et al., "Dissociative identity disorder and the sociocognitive model: Recalling lessons of the past," *Psychological Bulletin* 125 (1999), pp. 507–523.

Questions to Consider:

1. How would you ever know whether someone who was acting out multiple identities actually had dissociative identity disorder or was faking it?

2. What do you think is different about homosexuality that makes mental health professionals consider it an alternative lifestyle and not a paraphilia?

Lecture Nine—Transcript
Disorders of Brain, Body, Self, Drugs, Sex

This lecture is a continuation of the lectures we are having on the classifications of mental illness. As you will recall, we are using DSM-IV and going through the various classifications of mental illness. We talked considerably at length on classification systems and how they work. We have already been over a couple of these: we have talked about anxiety disorders and mood disorders. Today we are going to talk about five more disorders, so we are not going to be able to spend a whole lot of time on any particular disorder; so I will have to run through these fairly quickly. And the disorders we are going to talk about today are cognitive disorders, where there is actually some problem with the brain organically that causes behavioral problems. We are going to talk about somatoform disorders, which are disorders were there are bodily complaints that have a psychological root cause to them. And then we are going to talk about dissociative disorders, where this an integrated whole personality, but something breaks off from that personality in some way. We will then talk about substance-related disorders, drugs of abuse, and drugs you are exposed to, and what kind of effects those have. And finally we will talk about sexual disorders, which is a catchall category, as we will see; people who have problems with sexual functioning, and also people who have what is considered deviant sexual practices. That is what we are gong to try to do today.

The cognitive disorders are where there is an impairment of the brain; something has gone wrong. We will talk about some of the causes in a minute; can be due to old age, can be accidents, for example, and other kinds of diseases; and all of these can cause an organic problem with the brain that shows up as a behavior problem.

First we need to define a few terms so that we understand what these behavioral problems are. One term that we need to understand is delirium. Now we all sometimes use the word delirious. Delirium is defined as a disturbance of consciousness in some way. That disturbance can lead to things, like to confusion and disorientation, and the most frequent cause of it is drug intoxication or withdrawal—and this is particularly true for elderly. But it does not have to always be drug intoxication. For example, perhaps your parents or your grandparents have been out shopping or something like that and get lost and do not know where they are and are very confused and disoriented and cannot remember even why they are there. That would be an example of delirium.

A second definition is dementia. With dementia what you have are multiple cognitive deficits, and usually there is a deficit of the memory as part of dementia. Dementia, for example, is a major symptom of Alzheimer's disorder that we are going to talk about in some length in a minute or so.

The third thing that we need is amnestic disorders, and these are specific deficits in memory where there are not other cognitive impairments involved. So this would be a person who seems to have memory problems, but everything else seems to be pretty well intact.

Let us talk some about Alzheimer's disease, because it is a big one. It is part of the reason why "cognitive disorders" is a classification that has lots and lots of folks in it. The biggest subcategory of it is diseases of old age, and Alzheimer's is the biggest of those. About 56% of dementia cases in fact are Alzheimer's disease. You are probably familiar with Alzheimer's disease now because it is so prevalent in our society and so many people are dealing with parents or grandparents who are going through this. It is a slow progressing disease where there is a deteriorating health condition.

When I first started to lecture some 35 years ago or so, Alzheimer's disease was considered pretty exotic, and it was used only when talking, for the most part at least, about pre-senile disorders. Somebody would get this at say age 45 or 50, which was considered quite unusual. So there were not many cases of Alzheimer's, or at least they were not called that. They were called senility; and people, when they get to be 60, 70, 80 years old, who started losing brain function were just considered to be senile. They would typically die and there would not be an autopsy. So they did not realize that in fact it was Alzheimer's that had the same kind of symptomology that this early onset kind of senility also had. Now we know that if you in fact do an autopsy, you will see gross kinds of changes in the brain. So if you look at the brain itself, it will have kind of shriveled up, like it has been kept in salt water or something like that. All these nice fat convolutions on the outside of the brain will have withered away to some degree, and that would indicate Alzheimer's. And then you could also do it at the neurological level, where you go in and look at the micro level and you will see changes too. Apparently this is due to a protein plaque that forms on the brain and eventually kills the neurons of the brain; and so the brain, in fact, physically gets smaller and withers up due to this protein plaque.

About 4 million people in the U.S. currently have Alzheimer's disorder, and it is expected to triple this number in the next 50 years unless we find some way of curing Alzheimer's, and that is mainly because the demographics of the country are changing and people are living longer, and there is a huge sort of population bubble that is going in that direction, and with those folks, a lot of them will have Alzheimer's. It does increase—the probability increases—as a person gets older. In the 60s and 70s the numbers start to pick up; and then by the time people are in their 80s to 90s, about half the people have Alzheimer's disease at that point.

There is really no effective treatment for Alzheimer's disorder. People try various kinds of things. I just saw an ad on television this week for a psychopharmacological intervention, where there is a pill that is supposed to improve the person's memory that is having Alzheimer's. I am not sure about the clinical studies on that. They are selling it for that ad. It may have a slight improvement—I'm not sure, but not much. And they have tried various things. They have tried massive vitamins. They tried oxygen as a way of trying to keep the brain from shriveling up. We do know that some of this may be hereditary; people with Alzheimer's in the family tend to be more likely to have Alzheimer's. And we also know that there are some environmental kinds of things as well that influence this. People who are mentally active tend to do better. The proportion of people who get Alzheimer's, for those who are not mentally active and physically active for that matter, there is a larger proportion of people who get Alzheimer's with that.

The other causes of cognitive disorders, besides the diseases of old age and Alzheimer's, one of these is stroke, where there is a blockage of the blood supply to the brain and part of the brain loses its functionality; and physical therapy is supposed to retrain another part of the brain to do those functions. Parkinson's disease, and also brain injury—so somebody who is in an automobile accident, or somebody that has a gunshot wound to the head—they would fit into this category as well. The most frequently occurring amnestic syndrome that has symptoms of memory loss is chronic alcohol use.

All right, that is cognitive disorders. Let us move on to the second, and that is somatoform disorders. Now "soma" means body, so here we are talking about a disorder where there are complaints about bodily symptoms or deficits, and for which there is no corresponding organic or medical cause for these particular deficits. One of the sub-classifications here is hypochondriasis. This is a person who believes that he or she has a particular disease and they have symptoms associated with that disease; at least they report those symptoms. And yet, if you give them physical examinations, you will find no medical basis for this. So they may complain that they have heart palpitations and that they do not think their heart beats strongly enough and that it is irregular and they have this whole collection of symptoms; and they go to the doctor and the doctor gives them an EKG and does other tests on them and cannot find any problem with them. And they insist that they do have this problem.

Now hypochondriasis, if it is sort of a single disease that they are talking about here, and if it lasts for at least six months, according to the classification system, it is not somebody who just for a week or two complains about lower back pain or something like that. We are talking about somebody who for a considerable period of time thinks they have a major medical problem. So they are preoccupied by their bodily functions. Now these people can be helped to some extent by cognitive therapy, but they do not really want to go see a psychologist, because for them it is a real problem; they think they have a physical problem. They do not like people even suggesting that it is in their head somehow, but there is no real root cause to this problem. So they are very reluctant to go to try to get help for the problem.

A second form that looks a lot like hypochondriasis is somatization disorder. It is similar to hypochondriasis in that there are physical complaints. But in this case, there are multiple physical complaints, and so they may have, according to the classification system, they have to have a minimum of four pain symptoms; two gastrointestinal symptoms, one sexual symptom, and one pseudoneurological symptom. And they have to have all of that; and that might seem odd to you that you would have to have that much, but it is not that unusual.

I play a tape for my students of a fellow who has this diagnostic category. And this poor fellow, I mean he sounds like a commercial for painkillers on television. He complains about how his stomach hurts; his solar plexus are swollen up in the middle—he does not know much about the human body—and how his wrists hurt and how his back hurts from picking up his boy and how he has trouble sexually and how he has trouble digesting his food and he has constipation, and on and on about headaches. I mean he has everything that there is, and for 20 to 25 minutes, he goes on and on about these things. And you might think, this poor fellow, he is really in pretty bad shape. Then you discover that he has been going to the doctor, and in fact at the end of the tape he finally admits that on some days he would go see three different doctors on the same day, because he had all of these complaints and none of them could find anything wrong with him. So that is somatization disorder, where there are multiple complaints.

Pain disorder also fits into this category, where a person reports a pain that might be in some area or multiple areas of the body, and again, which there is no medical condition that they can discover for this. And this is a particularly difficult one to do. Pain is so subjective; how do you crawl inside someone else and find out whether they really have pain? And for these people, it certainly is pain. You cannot say, I deny the fact that you have pain; it is all in your head—they do not want to hear that at all—and yet they have a very difficult time often finding the diagnosis. So they do not attribute the problem to themselves, they attribute the problem to the incompetence of the doctors who are trying to find what is causing their pain, because their pain is very real for them

Conversion disorder. We did talk about conversion disorder already. Here when we talked about Freud, in fact, we talked about hysteria, which is the early name for conversion disorder, where you might have an arm that goes numb or you might have blindness for a period of time, and there is psychological causes to it rather than physical causes.

Finally, there is a sort of exotic one called body dysmorphic disorder, and this when somebody thinks that they have something wrong with their physical appearance and that it is so bad that they cannot have a proper relationship with somebody else. They think people at work are always looking at them because this ugly distortion they have in their body somehow. We have all had a little of this, I mean when I was growing up, I would look in the mirror and say, oh my nose is awful big and my ears stick out too far. So all of us sort of think that, but these are people who really think they are grotesque, yet they fit within the normal range of physical variability. And so that is called body dysmorphic disorder. So that is the somatoform disorders in the second category.

The third category we are going to look at is dissociative disorders. And if you picture somebody having a well-integrated self, and something becomes dissociated from that self, that is the general category here. An example of that is depersonalization, and in this case a person might think they do not even exist or that they are detached from reality somehow, on a temporary basis at least. Some people find that a very exotic thing to try to think about. I actually can resonate to that a little bit. If I go to visit a strange city and do not know anybody there and go for several days without talking to anybody and wander around the city and nobody pays any attention to me, every now and then I start feeling sort of weird, like maybe I am not even there. If you have had that experience, you are having just a little bit of this; but these people really do start to believe that they do not exist, and it is a far more serious disorder.

A second one is amnesia, and we are all pretty familiar with that. It is a memory loss of the events in a person's life or one's identity, and it has to last for a period of time. And again there is no physical precipitating event; they did not get a blow to the head or have some other traumatic thing happen to them. They just wake up one day and something is missing from their memory about their life.

Another subcategory here is fugue, and that means flight; and this would be exemplified by somebody who goes out to the grocery store to get a loaf of bread and never comes back. And two years later they find this person in a different location, moved to California, having a different life with very little memory of the life—that would be an example—and obviously dissociation from the previous life and the previous self.

Another one is identity disorder, and you have all heard of this. It used to be called multiple personality disorder or split personality. People get this confused with schizophrenia, because they know *schizo* means split and they think that must mean that there are multiple personalities, but it is a very different category as you see. It has nothing to do with schizophrenia. In this case people have identities that they switch often fairly frequently in the order of seconds, and one identity does not know the existence of the other identity there. It used to be considered a rather infrequent and unusual and exotic kind of a disorder until 1979. In fact there are only 200 reported cases of multiple personality disorder, or what is now called identity disorder. And they were so unusual that people wrote books about them. *The Three Faces of Eve*, and the 12 faces of somebody else; if you wanted to become a famous psychiatrist back in those days you would just write another book having a patient who had more identities than the last patient in the book. So it is quite unusual, but then by 1999, there had been reported over 30,000 cases of this disorder. Well, did people just start having this disorder? Well it is kind of controversial, because one of the things that happens is that there are a whole school of therapists that believe that women in particular who are having problems very often have been sexually assaulted or abused in the family situation when they were young, and that is the source of their problems, and that leads to this particular disorder, identity disorder, and they have to have identity disorder in this set of symptoms. And I am afraid that many of these therapists convinced their clients that they have multiple personalities, when in fact a lot of therapists believe that they do not. So it is kind of a controversial issue, and it is part of the reason that increased number is there.

Let us move on to the fourth category here, and that is substance-related disorders. And in this case it can refer to people who have drug abuse, but it can also refer to people who have had problems with medication, the side effects of medication, and to toxin exposure. We are going to talk at great length about drug abuse and the drugs that are used recreationally in a subsequent lecture. So let me just talk a little bit about this category. One subcategory includes the actual physiological impairments that people have from having prolonged and excessive use of a particular drug like alcohol. The one that people often cite is an alcohol abuse disorder called Korsakoff's syndrome. With Korsakoff's syndrome, the person has a memory problem, and it looks like that memory problem is a difficulty in transferring things from short-term memory--the kind of memory we use when we are trying to remember a phone number for 30 seconds or a minute—into long-term memory, the more permanent memory that we have throughout most of our lives. We automatically transfer that–particularly with rehearsal—that it goes into long term memory. Somebody with Korsakoff's syndrome seems to have lost the ability to do that.

I have a tape of a fellow with Korsakoff's syndrome. This fellow is about 70 years old, so he maybe getting some problems with Alzheimer's as well, but on this tape he talks about—he works in various breweries around Cincinnati, and at the time the tape was made there were lots of breweries around there. He claims he drank mostly beer, but he drank a lot of beer and he would get the shakes, although he claimed that he did not get the delirium tremens where he would see bugs and that sort of thing, but he did drink a lot. During the interview, the interviewer, who is a psychiatrist, at one point asks him, "And what is my name?" And he says, "Your name is Harry." And then he goes on for a while, and two minutes later the interviewer asks him again, "What did you say my name was?" And he says, "Your name is Happy." Then the phone rings about five minutes later and he sets it down and says, "What did you say my name was?" And he says, "Your name is Bob." So he was changing it every time, and that characterized—he would do what is sometimes called confabulation, make up pieces that sort of fit in where he had memory deficits. So if you talked to this guy for 30 seconds he sounds like he is fairly normal, but if you talked to him for as much as five minutes you will realize he has forgotten what he has told you just two minutes ago; and that is a characteristic of Korsakoff's syndrome.

A second major category is addictive disorders due to the use of a particular substance. And the person uses this substance, and it is a pathological use that results in hazardous behavior. And continued use of the substance can bring on very great negative consequences, and we are going to talk about that a bit more. Substance dependence occurs when you have a physiological need for a substance to the point where tolerance develops; that is, you need more and more of the particular substance to get the desired affect. So these are all substance-related disorders and fit in that category.

Let us talk about the final category here, and that is sexual and gender identity disorders. There are several subcategories that are really quite different from each other in this overall category. The first are sexual dysfunctions; and this means that somebody is having a difficult time performing the way they would like to be—sexually active and healthy. And you might ask, why is that one of the classifications of mental illness? Is this person really mentally ill? If this person wants to go get some help from a sex therapist or something like that, they have to have a classification; so it fits in here so that they can convince their insurance company to go talk to a therapist, and that is why it fits here. It does not mean that the person is crazy or anything, just because you have an erectile dysfunction. It does not mean that you are having a severe mental problem at all, but it has to fit in the classification system here. So some of these sexual dysfunctions include things like hyposexual desire—not hypersexual—hyposexual desire in which there is little interest in sex and sexual aversion, in which you want to avoid sexual contact all together. So if a person were having that kind of problem, you would be diagnosed this way and would go see a therapist about it if it is severe enough. Sexual arousal problems and dysfunctions there, such as male erectile disorder, which was at one time called impotence; or female sexual arousal disorder, which is formerly called frigidity. So if there is a problem with that, one could see a therapist about it.

There are also dysfunctions having to do with orgasm. In males, the usual complaint is premature ejaculation. And again, one might see a therapist about that particular problem. And in women the complaint is usually one of an inability to achieve orgasm, although that can be a complaint of both sexes as well. And there are also pain disorders where a person reports having severe pain when they try to have intercourse. So if the person had any of these particular disorders, this classification would allow them to go get some help for these disorders.

Also fitting under sexual and gender identity disorders are what are called the paraphilias. The paraphilias are characterized by frequent sexual urges, fantasies, or behaviors involving unusual objects, activities, or situations that cause distress. And I should point out here—I did earlier in this course—but I will point out again that homosexuality is not one of the subcategories here. Back in 1973, the

American Psychiatric Association took homosexuality out as a subcategory of the paraphilias. It is now considered to be an appropriate alternative lifestyle, and is no longer considered a disorder.

But some of those that are considered disorders are things like fetishism, and that is the case where a person receives sexual gratification from the use of an inanimate object, such as an article of clothing, a body part which is not usually considered sexually arousing. These would be fetishes, and there are all sorts of these, an unbelievable number of different kinds of fetishes that people have that seem unusual to folks who do not have those fetishes.

Another one is transvestic fetishism. People are sometimes called transvestites, and this involves a man receiving sexual gratification by dressing in women's clothing. This is kind of an unusual one, because this is a case where—if you will recall back when we were talking about what is the definition of abnormal behavior, we said very often one of the criteria is how socially acceptable it is. In our society, women are allowed to wear men's clothing, aren't they? When I look out at my class of 200 students 90% of the women are dressed in clothes that I could wear. They are wearing pants and a shirt or something like that; in today's society that is considered quite acceptable. But if I wore a skirt to class, people would say I have transvestic fetishism.

I had a colleague at my former university who taught sexual behavior, and once a semester he would wear a skirt to campus and walk around campus quite proudly in this skirt just to see what people's reaction is, to point out the absurdity of the fact that we have this rule that men cannot do this and that women can. But that is part of the way abnormal behavior is defined. I play a tape of a fellow who has transvestic fetishism to my class, and this is a 17-year-old young man who in fact derives great pleasure out of dressing up as a woman. In fact, he goes a little bit farther and even sometimes performs as a female impersonator. But he feels much more comfortable when he is dressed as a woman and he says he really feels more like a woman; and we will talk about the possibility in a minute that he also has gender identity disorder with this particular set of problems that he has, because that is not necessarily typical. More typically a guy works in a factory all day and comes home, and in the privacy of his own home gets out female clothing and puts it on, and he gets some sexual gratification out of that. So that is transvestic fetishism.

Voyeurism, what we sometimes call peeping, occurs when a man receives sexual gratification from observing an unsuspecting woman in a state of undress or in sexual activity. Exhibitionism is the opposite of that, that is when somebody derives sexual pleasure out of exposing ones genitals or being nude in front of somebody else. Again, I mention that when we were talking about abnormal behavior.

Sadism, which involves receiving sexual gratification out of inflicting pain on somebody else; and the opposite of that, masochism, which is receiving sexual gratification out of having pain inflicted upon you. Frotteurism involves sexual pleasure from touching or rubbing against somebody else who does not consent to that activity. Pedophilia—I think we are all familiar with that—that is sexual activity with a child. And then there are some even more exotic ones that have to do with corpses and animals and so forth. So these are all paraphilias, what we usually consider to be deviant kinds of sexual practices. It is very much tied up in the moral criteria and the social criteria of abnormality.

Finally, there is gender identity disorder, in which the person has a strong desire to be, really, the opposite sex. They feel like they have been inappropriately assigned their gender, and this may lead in some cases to actual operations to do gender change as well.

So today, we have been over five different categories of the DSM-IV. Talked about cognitive disorders, where there is an actual brain problem due to accidents or due to diseases. We talked about somatoform disorder, where there are complaints about the body or even the perception of the body and whether this is appropriate, and for which there are no medical kinds of conditions that should cause those complaints. We talked about dissociative disorder, where there is some dissociation from an integrated whole where a person might have a problem with memory, or other problems of multiple personality or something like that, where there is a dissociation. We talked some about substance related disorders, where the person is ingesting something that is not good for them over a prolonged period of time. And finally we talked about sexual disorders, both where there are complaints about sexual performance and where people seem to have a deviancy in terms of the sexual behavior that they have. Those are the five categories of mental illness. Thank you.

Lecture Ten
Schizophrenic Disorders

Scope:

Schizophrenia is a psychotic disorder in which there is a break with reality and such positive symptoms as delusions (false beliefs), hallucinations (false perceptions), and disorganized speech and behaviors. Negative symptoms include emotional flattening, lessened speech, and deficient will. Schizophrenia occurs in 1% of the population, most often in late adolescence to early adulthood and, in men, earlier and more severely. The primary symptom for paranoid schizophrenia is persecutory delusions. In disorganized schizophrenia, there is not only disorganized behavior but also inappropriate emotions. Catatonic schizophrenia is usually associated with fixed posturing. Undifferentiated type is a catchall category, and residual type is for those who have been schizophrenic but do not currently exhibit positive symptoms. Although the specific causes of schizophrenia are still uncertain, there is evidence of genetic involvement, prenatal involvement, and anatomical and neuronal involvement, as well as family environmental influences.

Outline

I. *Schizophrenia* is a psychotic disorder or, more probably, a set of disorders, in which there is a break with reality, as well as other symptoms.

    A. Schizophrenia includes positive symptoms, in which there is an excess or distortion of normal behavior.

        1. *Delusions* are false beliefs that are held even in the face of contradictory evidence (for example, "I am the king of Prussia"), experienced by about 90% of schizophrenic patients.

        2. *Hallucinations* are sensory events, usually auditory in nature for schizophrenia, for which there are no precipitating physical stimuli, experienced by about 75% of schizophrenic patients.

        3. Schizophrenic patients also often have disorganized speech, in which they fail to make sense, even to the point of making up their own words, called *neologisms*.

    4. Patients also usually have disorganized behavior in such areas as hygiene, dress, health, and personal interactions, and in the extreme case, they may exhibit catatonic behavior in the form of postural immobility.

B. Schizophrenia also includes negative symptoms, in which there is an absence of normally occurring behaviors, such as a flattening of emotions, lessened speech (*alogia*), and deficient will (*avolition*).

C. Many factors influence the likelihood of the onset of schizophrenia.

    1. Schizophrenia occurs in about 1% of the population.

    2. The most frequent onset time of the disorder is late adolescence to early adulthood, but this varies some with gender.

    3. Schizophrenia occurs earlier in men than women and is usually more severe in men.

    4. Children born to older fathers have a higher risk.

II. There are several different subtypes of schizophrenia, and these may, in fact, be different diseases.

A. In *paranoid-type* schizophrenic patients, the major symptom, besides a break with reality, is a pervasive belief that they are being persecuted.

    1. The persecutory delusions are often quite elaborate, involving convoluted stories of multiple enemies and delusions of grandeur.

    2. Cognitive functioning of this subtype is usually higher than other subtypes, and the prognosis for recovery is often better.

B. *Disorganized type*, which was once called *hebephrenic schizophrenia*, occurs earlier and more gradually and involves symptoms of disorganized behavior and speech and inappropriate emotions.

    1. In this subtype, the inappropriate emotions are often characterized by inappropriate laughter and giggling.

    2. Hallucinations or delusions may be present but are not elaborate or organized.

    3. Bizarre behaviors are often present.

4. Prognosis for disorganized-type schizophrenia is poor, and patients are often institutionalized for long periods.

C. *Catatonic-type schizophrenic* patients appear to become unresponsive to the world around them, either by going into a stupor and maintaining a fixed posture or by becoming quite excited and agitated, much like the manic phase of a bipolar patient.

D. *Undifferentiated schizophrenia* is a catchall category for those who exhibit many of the symptoms of schizophrenia but do not fit neatly into one of the other subtypes.

E. People with *residual-type schizophrenia* have at one time had schizophrenia but are not currently showing any severe positive symptoms, although negative symptoms are still present.

III. The precise cause of schizophrenia is unknown although a number of factors influence the disorder and can help us infer what the cause or causes may be.

A. There is a clear genetic connection, apparent from studies in which the percentage of incidence of schizophrenia was determined for someone related in various ways to a relative with schizophrenia, as follows: identical twins, about 50%; first-degree relative (such as a sibling), about 10%; second-degree relative (such as a nephew or niece), about 5%; third-degree relative (such as a first cousin), about 2%.

B. Genetic studies have shown that at least four chromosomes might contain genes that are related to schizophrenia.

C. The prenatal environment also appears to be related to the incidence of schizophrenia in later life, with viral infections, Rh blood incompatibility with the mother, malnutrition, and delivery problems all implicated.

D. Brain volume is related to schizophrenia in some but not all patients.

E. Neurons in the central nervous system communicate by means of chemicals called *neurotransmitters*, and several of these, such as dopamine and glutamate, are related to schizophrenia.

F. The degree of emotional tension in families has also been shown to be related to how often schizophrenic patients return to the hospital.

Essential Reading:

James Butcher, Susan Mineka, and Jill Hooley, *Abnormal Psychology*, 12th ed., chapter 14.

Supplementary Reading:

American Psychiatric Association, *Diagnostic and Statistical Manual of Mental Disorders*, 4th ed.

I. I. Gottesman, "Psychopathology through a life span-genetic prism," *American Psychologist* 56 (2001), pp. 867–878.

Mark Vonnegut, *The Eden Express*.

Questions to Consider:

1. In the word *schizophrenia*, *schizo* does mean "split," but if the split is not split personalities (as in dissociative identity disorder), what is being split?

2. If schizophrenia were an entirely genetic disorder, then identical twins, who are 100% genetically related, should always both be schizophrenic or not, but we know that when one is schizophrenic, the other is schizophrenic only 50% of the time. Why?

Lecture Ten—Transcript
Schizophrenic Disorders

In this lecture we are continuing our discussion of the various mental disorders and you will recall that we are using DMS-IV to go through the mental disorders and look at the various symptoms and other information about these disorders. Today, we are going to talk about schizophrenia. This is a very important disorder. You may recall when we looked at the incidences of various mental disorders that schizophrenia only comprised about 1% of the population has schizophrenia. That may seem like a small number, however, the severity of the disorder is such that it is one of the major disorders that we have to be concerned about. People are hospitalized at very high rates for schizophrenia and so a lot of the resources in this country that go to mental health field go because of schizophrenia. Many of the hospital beds in our mental hospitals go to schizophrenic patients.

So today we are going to talk about schizophrenia, we will talk first about the symptoms of schizophrenia, what defines this as a disorder and we are going to talk some about the various subtypes of schizophrenia. In fact, there are those who would argue that schizophrenia is not a single category, it is a collection of subtypes of schizophrenia and those subtypes might have different root causes. And finally, we are going to talk some about the possible causes of schizophrenia and we do not have surefire answers yet, but we have data that suggests what some of the possible causes of schizophrenia might be. So that is what we are going to do today.

Schizophrenia is a psychotic disorder and by psychosis we mean, generally, that there is a break with reality. Somehow the person is no longer in touch with the external world in one way or another. And when there is a break with reality, there are other psychosis although schizophrenia is the largest disorder where there is a break with reality where there is psychosis and one of the ways that you might try to determine whether there is a break with reality is if you were talking to somebody to try to a diagnosis, you might ask them person, place and time orientation questions. Who are you? Do they know who there are? Do they think they are Napoleon instead of who they actually are? Do they know where they are? Do they realize that they are in a mental hospital or do they realize what city they are in, or, they may think they are in a different country all together. Do they know what time it is? Not the time of day but do they know even what era they are living in? If they think they are Napoleon, they make think they are in a different century even. So, person, place and time orientation is one of the main ways of trying to determine whether somebody has a psychotic disorder. With schizophrenia very often there are deficits in their person, place and time orientation.

There are what is sometimes called positive symptoms and also negative symptoms of schizophrenia. That does not mean that the positive symptoms are good things to have and that the negative symptoms are bad things to have. The positive refers to behaviors that are added over and above what are considered to be normal behaviors and the negative symptoms are behaviors that are subtracted from what are considered to be normal kinds of behaviors.

So we will go over some of those symptoms. First let me make a point that I made in a previous lecture, but I think it is worth making again. People think that schizophrenia, because schizo means a split of some sort often think that schizophrenia has to do with split personalities and that is simply not the case. As we learned in the last lecture, split personalities or multiple personalities are now called dissociative identity disorders and that is a completely different category from schizophrenia. So what does split mean? Well split means a split of partly because there is a break with reality so they have split with reality but there is also a split of the emotions from reality. Throughout the subcategories when we go over them, you will see that in many of the subcategories there is inappropriate emotion as part of what you are getting with that subcategory, so that is the split; the emotion from reality.

The positive symptoms are those things that have been added to normal behavior. Delusions are a very frequent positive symptom. In fact about 90% of schizophrenic patients exhibit some form of delusion. These are false beliefs. They believe that perhaps they are the King of Prussia or something like that when in fact that there is no evidence to indicate they are the King of Prussia. So those would be a delusion of grandeur where they think they are more important. Perhaps they think they are Jesus Christ. Those would all be delusions and they do not have to be delusions that are quite so large, they might believe that people can see into their heads. That is always a fear of many schizophrenics. They are afraid that people can read their minds and that terrifies them because they have all of these what they think are strange thoughts and they think other people can see that they have strange thoughts. They might have delusions that they are hearing things, in which case we would call it a hallucination.

Hallucinations in this case, we have sensory events that are usually auditory in nature. I always thought that when I first read about hallucinations in schizophrenics that they were seeing things like ghosts. More frequently it is that they are hearing voices, hearing voices in their heads and hallucinations occur in about 75% of schizophrenic patients. People report that these voices are very real to them. Some people describe it as if there were a radio sitting in their head playing and talking to them and they hear these voices and these voices can be very commanding. Sometimes usually actually the voices are saying rather negative things to them. Like you are no good and telling them how bad they are and they have to listen to this all the time; they cannot get away from it. Sometimes when you see schizophrenic patients who seem to have nothing going on they are sort of standing there not doing anything and you ask them to report what is going on; they will report that there is a lot of activity and it is all happening in their head and they have to spend all of their attention on what is going on in their head and cannot even interact with the environment for that reason. So hallucinations are a primary positive symptom of schizophrenia.

Disorganized speech is another symptom of schizophrenia. That is one that I think is often is diagnostic before the person might have extreme delusions or hallucinations. You will hear people when you talk to them who are just bordering on schizophrenia, starting to have speech patterns that are very unusual. There is a tape I play my students of a paranoid schizophrenic and I will describe her a little more later and one of the things she does is use speech in a strange way and she even uses what is called neologisms. Neologisms are making up words that are not real words or using words in their speech, they also use words that rhyme with each other. She in fact describes her parents came from Bellefontaine, Ohio, you know that, that is where Grandpa Bell's Fountains were she said and then later on she is talking about the Liberty Bell and how they ring the Liberty

Bell, hear ye hear ye and gather around and she is talking about the bell, referring to the Statue of Liberty in the harbor and talking about her grandpa Bell and using this word in sort of this strange way and often even rhyming it while she is doing this. So she makes up words, neologisms, she rhymes words and you will see people doing this very frequently as they are entering into schizophrenia.

Patients also have disorganized behavior quite frequently in terms of their hygiene, in terms of the way they dress, their health, their personal interactions with people, and in the extreme case they might have even catatonic behavior. We will talk about that as a subclassification in a minute where they have postural immobility, where they do not even move. So those are some of the positive symptoms of schizophrenia, those are things that are added to normal behavior that you would not usually see. Then there is a whole collection of what are negative symptoms as well. There seems to be a dichotomy here, the positive and the negative symptoms. Once we give people and we will talk a little bit later about therapies for schizophrenia one of the major therapies are antipsychotic drugs that they take and at least the older antipsychotic drugs one of the problems was they were pretty good at getting rid of the positive symptoms, people had fewer delusions and no longer hallucinated. But in fact the negative symptoms were still there. So it may be a different kind of collection of things we have with the positive symptoms and the negative symptoms.

Some of the negative symptoms include absence of normally occurring behaviors, such as a flattening of emotions, lessening speech, which is sometimes called alogia, deficit in will which is sometimes called avolition where the person cannot even get motivated to act in a particular way. And in general we could describe this as an apathetic or withdrawn kind of personality at this point. So in addition to having some of these more exotic positive symptoms, they also sometimes have this flattening of emotions and withdrawal and apathy kind of thing that is going on, that we call the negative symptoms.

Now let us look at some of the factors that influence the likelihood of somebody getting schizophrenia. We already mentioned that schizophrenia affects about 1% of the population. We also know that schizophrenia comes on, the onset is usually around late adolescence to early adulthood. My college students are often interested in finding that out that they are in prime time for the possibility of getting schizophrenia. I had a friend and fraternity brother when I was in school, who seemed to be a normal kind of guy, he would act a little strange from time to time but nothing so out of the ordinary that he was not considered a pretty good friend to us. He went home for holiday break one year and started acting oddly and he never came back to school. He was diagnosed with schizophrenia and was in and out of hospitals for the rest of his life. He is now dead in fact. He died about seven years ago and had a diagnosis of schizophrenia. So that is kind of the time it most likely occurs. However there are differences between men and women in this regard. Men tend to get schizophrenia earlier and they tend to get it more severely than women do. If you look at a graph with age across the bottom and you plot it with a bar showing men and women in the 20s into the 30s, you will see men considerably above the women in terms of the incidences of schizophrenia. Then around 30 or so, the graph changes and more women start getting schizophrenia at that point and that increases in fact, all the way into the age of 60 or so, that women get more schizophrenia than men do.

It has been hypothesized that it might be due to estrogen and as menopause occurs and the estrogen levels change. Estrogen perhaps is having some positive effect in preventing schizophrenia. We are not sure that is the case but that is a hypothesis at least at this point. Children born to older fathers are also of higher risk for getting schizophrenia. Later in this lecture we will talk some about heredity of schizophrenia as well.

Let us talk some about the subtypes of schizophrenia and I already mentioned that these subtypes might be different diseases themselves. We are not quite sure. The one that is probably the most prominent, the one that I tend to see if you go into a mental institution and see more people with this subclassification is paranoid type schizophrenia. Now I think you probably know what the word paranoid means. Someone who is paranoid think that folks are out to get them, that people are plotting against them, perhaps people are opening their mail and reading it and so forth and we will see later on when we talk about personality disorders that there is a whole disorder called paranoid personalities. So just because you have paranoia does not mean you are schizophrenic, you have to have these other symptoms as well, things like delusions and hallucinations and it has to be pretty strong. This is one subcategory and these people have a pervasive belief that they are being persecuted and these persecutory delusions are often quite elaborate involving convoluted stories of multiple enemies and delusions of grandeur.

This woman who was on the tape that I mentioned just a minute ago who had paranoid schizophrenia she talked about how the confusionists were out get her. Confusionist is a neologism, a word she made up, that the confusionists were out to get her and that they were British confusionists who were at here day and night, she said and they were trying to rape her and they were trying to kill her relatives and she went through this huge story. If you think that mentally ill people are sort of dull and dimwitted, you should listen to a paranoid schizophrenic for a while. Her mind is racing just as fast as it can. She is going through this story faster than she can get the words out and you are sitting there with your eyes wide open just listening to this story and in no way is she dull or unintelligent, but gives you this elaborate kind of story.

When I was in undergraduate school and took abnormal and clinical psychology we would go visit a mental institution, a local mental institution, and we were assigned our own patients to interview. We would go in three times a week and do this over about a four-week period of time. I had one fellow who was a paranoid schizophrenic who I would talk to; interesting fellow, and what I discovered is not only did he these elaborate stories but the stories changed from day to day when I would go in to talk to him. He had a military background so many of the stories had a military kind of flavor to them. But one day I would go in and he would tell me how he was a military chaplain. He would tell me about all the folks that he helped while he was a military chaplain and then the next day I would go in and he had invented the airplane and he was a very important person in the military because he invented the airplane and he would go on and on about that. So very creative but he certainly was paranoid because there then was a theme running through these stories about people who were out to get him and that is why he was locked up after all. He had done nothing wrong; he was locked up because he was a political prisoner as many paranoid schizophrenic patients think they are when they are in a mental institution. In fact the paranoid schizophrenics in mental institutions often are convincing enough that there gets to be kind of a lore in a mental institution and everybody picks up a little bit of the paranoia and thinks that there is arsenic in the drinking fountains, bodies are being stuffed down the sewer at night and that sort of thing. It is just sort of a general belief people pick up who are in mental institutions because there are so many people with these kinds of stories.

So they have persecutory delusions and their cognitive functioning is usually higher as I mentioned in this type of schizophrenia. Another subtype of schizophrenia is the disorganized type and this used to be called hebephrenia or hebephrenic schizophrenia and it occurs earlier and more gradually than something like paranoid schizophrenia and involves symptoms of disorganized behavior and speech and also inappropriate emotions.

I play a tape for my students of somebody with disorganized schizophrenia, somebody who has been in a mental institution at that time for 30 years and in fact for disorganized type while the symptoms are not quite so pronounced and severe, the prognosis is poorer than for paranoid schizophrenics. Paranoid schizophrenics often do recover some from their condition. Disorganized schizophrenic patients often do not. So she had been in the institution for 30 years. At the time she was not displaying a lot of hallucinations or delusions, she was taking some medication that were probably blunting those to some extent but she still had some of the other behaviors that are characteristic of this disorganized type. In her case, the most noticeable thing was her inappropriate laughter and giggling. She would be telling her story and telling a story about for example she would say well I've been in this institution. The doctor who was interviewing her said well do you have any kids. She says well I guess I have some kids [laughter]. I thought I had one kid [laughter] they told me I had two kids [laughter] and she would do this kind of laughing. Well are you going to get out, well I certainly hope so [laughter]. Just this sort of strange kind of laughing and inappropriate emotional connection, the kind of things she is talking about and that is a common characteristic of disorganized type of schizophrenia.

So inappropriate emotions, laughter and giggling, there may be hallucinations and delusions—in her case they were no longer there—but they are not the elaborate, organized kind of thing that you see with a paranoid schizophrenic. There is also sometimes bizarre behavior. When she was put into the institution, 30 years before, part of the reason they put her in is she was tearing off her clothing and yelling and screaming and acting in a very bizarre way.

The next category or subcategory is catatonic type schizophrenia, what is sometimes called catatonia, and these patients are generally unresponsive to the world around them. The way we are most familiar with it is when they go into a stupor and maintain a fixed posture that is sometimes called statue-like posturing and it sometimes has what is called waxy flexibility. It means they are kind of like a mannequin and you can move them around—they are flexible—so they are standing there like this and not having any kind of emotion and you can walk over and grab their arm and hold it up and they would assume that posture like they were a mannequin. They will stand there for minutes and sometimes for hours at a time in that posture you put them in. Again, people thought, well they just shut down completely, but when they talk to these people about what goes on while they are in this catatonic state, again they will say things are just rushing through their mind and it is all they can do to just to pay attention to their mind and so it is not that their mind has shut down, it is kind of like the body has shut down and separated itself from their mind. People who have this subcategory sometimes have the opposite of that and are excited and agitated and resemble the manic phase of bipolar disorder that we talked about in a previous lecture.

Then there is a category that is not very exciting called undifferentiated schizophrenia in which there are—it is kind of a catchall category—and they have the general symptoms of schizophrenia but it does not fit cleanly into any of the other subclassifications.

Finally, there is the category called residual type schizophrenia and this is a person who at one time had all of the kinds of symptoms that we would expect to have of schizophrenia, but in recent times are not showing the severe positive symptoms, although the negative symptoms are still present. I play a tape of a fellow who has this categorization, too. He had been in the mental institution for 32 years. He became schizophrenic when he was 17 and started having trouble in school and then had a break with reality and they put him in the institution. At the time they interviewed him, he had been in there for so long that he had developed an institutionalized kind of personality. He was willing to admit to anything. He talked in kind of a low monotone in the interview, very little emotion; that is the negative side of things, his apathy and withdrawal. He was willing to agree to anything you would say. The fellow who was interviewing him said, "And what was your father's name?" He says, "Ted, I think." "You are not sure what your father's name was?" "No." He says well, "maybe your father was named Frank." "Yeah, could be." "Or, maybe George. Could it be George?" "Yeah, could be." "Maybe it was Rudolph, was it Rudolph?" "Yeah, could be." "Well, what was your father's name?" "Well, it was Fred." "Then why did you say at the beginning these other kinds of things?"

This fellow had been in there for so long he was just trying to get along. He was institutionalized, if you had let him out of the institution, he would have been totally incapable of dealing with the world at that point. So he had this residual type, he still had these negative kind of symptoms of schizophrenia but no longer was displaying the positive symptoms.

What are the reasons for schizophrenia? What is the cause of schizophrenia? As I mentioned earlier, we only have an inkling of what that might be at this point. If I had been teaching this course 50 years ago, at this point when I was trying to talk about the cause of schizophrenia, I would have told you what was the prevailing attitude at the time. Schizophrenia is caused by cold and uncaring parents; mothers in particular. It is their fault. And that is kind of the blank slate notion, if we go back to what I talked about earlier on in this course about the blank slate and how the behaviorist held sway at that point and that everything was written on it. Well, if you do not have a brain disorder, if nothing is built in there to give you schizophrenia, it must be due to the environment. If people are getting schizophrenia in their late adolescence, their environment is pretty much their family, so let us blame the family for it since we do not know. So that is what I would have been teaching you. It is absolutely wrong. We know that is not the case, there is no correlation between cold and uncaring mothers and schizophrenia.

So what is the cause? Well, we do know that there is a clear genetic connection. We know that though inheritability studies, where you go in and you take a person who has schizophrenia and then you try to find out how likely it is that somebody else who has a particular relationship with that person has schizophrenia. If you do that, you find that for identical twins, you would expect that to be the most—if it is somewhat inherited—you would expect that identical twins would have a close correspondence of having schizophrenia. Indeed, if one identical twin has schizophrenia, the likelihood of the other one having it is about 50%, which is very high. Now this tells you that it is not absolutely deterministic this way, because otherwise it would be a 100%, because genetically they are alike. With an identical twin I am sure you know that you have an egg that was fertilized by a single sperm and then later that split and so the genetics of these identical twins are exactly alike. So, if it was entirely genetic, both of them would have it 100% of the time. So it is not 100% deterministic this way. So that does tell us, however, that there is a strong genetic hereditary predisposition to schizophrenia.

If you get folks who are not quite so related, first-degree relatives—those are people like siblings or your brothers and your sisters—it drops down to about 10%. If one has schizophrenia, the likelihood of the other one having it would be about 10% as opposed to, remember, that in the general population it is 1%. So it is 10 times more likely than you would be to have it just by being in the general population. Second-degree relatives such as nephews, where the relationship is down to a genetic relationship of about .25, we are down to about 5%. Third-degree relatives, such as first cousins, we are down to about 2%.

Then there are also relationships in terms of, for example, if both parents have schizophrenia, it is around 50% again. So there is a relationship that way as well. We also know from research on adopted children that the environment is not nearly the kind of predictor that heredity is. If you have identical twins, who were raised separately—now there is not a whole lot of data on that—it is a fairly small number of people that you can find with that situation, but if they were identical twins and raised separately, it makes almost no difference in terms of how likely they are to get schizophrenia, it is still about 50%.

So, in that way, the environment probably is not nearly so strong as the genetic connection. We do know by doing genetic studies that at least four chromosomes might contain genes that are related to schizophrenia. We know that schizophrenia is undoubtedly a polygenic trait; that means that there are multiple genes that are determining this. Back when I was first lecturing I predicted that within 15 years we would have a cure for schizophrenia because I thought we would have made enough progress with genetic engineering that we could go in there and tweak that gene and get rid of schizophrenia. It turns out that it is located in multiple places in the genetic code and we are probably—if we are going to do that kind of work—have to go get it in multiple places. It is not a single gene that is causing schizophrenia.

We do know that the prenatal environment has something to do with schizophrenia as well. That things like viral infections, Rh blood incompatibility with the mother, malnutrition, and even delivery problems can cause a higher incidence of schizophrenia. We also know something that brain volume—perhaps you have read about people with schizophrenia have larger ventricles in their brains—and it is true some of them do and it is somewhat of a predictor, but then it is not a perfect predictor either. Not all schizophrenic patients have larger ventricles in their brain. So brain size does not predict it entirely.

We know that it has something to do with the neurotransmitter substances, too. We are going to talk more about that in a future lecture. We have neurotransmitters substance by which neurons talk to each other. We know that dopamine and glutamate are related to schizophrenia. Finally, we also know that there is some environmental affect. That if you take a person with schizophrenia who gets out of the hospital, and goes back into a situation where there is a lot of emotional tension in the family situation, that they are more likely to go back into the institution than if they go into a more placid environment. So we know that the environment has something to do with it, but it is probably not a major driver.

So that is a quick overview of schizophrenia. What we talked about today are the symptoms of schizophrenia, both the positive and the negative symptoms. We then also dealt with some of the subtypes of schizophrenia, such as paranoid, disorganized type, catatonic, undifferentiated, and residual type schizophrenia and finally we talked briefly about some of the possible causes of schizophrenia. Thank you.

Lecture Eleven
Childhood, Retardation, Personality Disorders

Scope:

Disorders usually diagnosed in infancy, childhood, or adolescence constitute a large category containing many learning, motor-skills, and communication problems experienced by children. One of the largest of these is attention-deficit/hyperactivity disorder, in which the child has impulsivity and overactivity problems. It occurs in up to 5% of children—much more frequently in boys—leads to lowered IQ scores, and is sometimes medicated by Ritalin. Autistic children seem to be cut off from the external world, have problems with social skills and speech, and engage in self-stimulation. Those with Tourette's syndrome have uncontrollable vocal and motor outbursts. Mental retardation is the diagnosis for someone under 18 years old who has significantly subaverage intelligence and limitations on functioning. It can be caused by genetic factors, infections and toxic agents, birth traumas, radiation, or dietary deficiencies. The degrees of severity are largely defined by IQ ranges and vary from mild, in which sixth-grade academic skills and self-support are possible, through moderate, severe, and profound, in which constant supervision and custodial care are necessary. Personality disorders are relatively permanent and inflexible patterns of interpersonal difficulties and problems with the sense of self that are categorized as paranoid, schizoid, schizotypal, antisocial, borderline, histrionic, narcissistic, avoidant, dependent, and obsessive-compulsive.

Outline

I. Disorders usually first diagnosed in infancy, childhood, or adolescence constitute a category that includes many learning, motor-skills, and communication disorders experienced by children for which parents might seek help, as well as some other notable disorders that we will discuss in more detail.

    A. With *attention-deficit/hyperactivity disorder* (ADHD) the child has impulsivity and overactivity that interfere with schoolwork and interpersonal relations.

1. ADHD occurs in about 3% to 5% of school-aged children and is 6 to 9 times more prevalent in boys than girls.
2. Evolutionary psychology offers an explanation for ADHD in that our ancestors' children would have been physically active all day and not forced to sit still in a school room, behavior that is, from an evolutionary standpoint, unnatural.
3. Because of their behavior problems, children with ADHD test 7 to 15 points lower on IQ tests.
4. The question of whether ADHD continues beyond adolescence is somewhat controversial.
5. The most frequently prescribed medication for ADHD is Ritalin, which is found to be effective in about 75% of cases; ironically, Ritalin is an amphetamine, a stimulant.

B. With *autism*, children seem to cut themselves off from the external world, causing deficits in language, perception, and motor development, as well as difficulties functioning in social situations.
1. Autism occurs in 5 to 7 children out of every 10,000 and is 2 to 4 times more prevalent in boys than girls.
2. Autistic children seem to lack the ability to empathize, to put themselves in other people's places, and this inability leads to very poor social skills.
3. Without massive training, autistic children have severe deficits in speech and engage in such behaviors as *echolalia*, the parrot-like repeating of words and phrases.
4. Autistic children also engage in self-stimulation, such as spinning or rocking, and sometimes self-destructive behaviors, such as head banging.
5. Autistic children show significant intellectual deficits but sometimes have special abilities in a narrowly defined cognitive area. Such children are known as *savants*.
6. Medications have proved largely ineffective for autism. However, behavior therapies (which will be discussed in a future lecture) can be effective in bringing behaviors closer to a normal range.
7. Some adult autistic advocacy groups are now arguing that autism should not be treated as a mental disorder but

that autistic individuals should be considered as having different talents and ways of behaving.

C. *Tourette's syndrome* is a tic disorder in which there can be inappropriate movements and vocal behaviors.

    1. Those with Tourette's syndrome seem to have a build-up of tension that is relieved by an outburst that may include shouts, snorts, yelps, or words.

    2. In about one-third of the cases, the vocal outburst may include speaking obscenities.

    3. Tourette's syndrome usually begins around the age of 7 and lasts into adulthood.

    4. Antipsychotic medications are sometimes effective, and behavioral therapies also sometimes show positive effects.

II. *Mental retardation* is the classification for someone under 18 years of age who has significantly subaverage intelligence and significant limitations in adaptive functioning in at least two areas, such as communication, self-care, academic skills, work, or health and safety.

A. Mental retardation can be caused by many factors.

    1. Genetic factors are apparent in that mental retardation tends to run in families and in such conditions as Down syndrome, which is particularly prevalent for older mothers and fathers and is attributable to an extra chromosome.

    2. Infections and toxic agents can increase the probability of mental retardation, such as prenatal German measles and alcohol intoxication.

    3. Physical birth traumas, such as insufficient oxygen, can also cause mental retardation.

    4. Although less frequent today than in the past, radiation, such as exposure to x-rays, may also be implicated.

    5. Finally, prenatal dietary deficiencies can cause deficits.

B. The degrees of severity are defined by intelligence quotient (IQ) levels.

    1. With mild mental retardation (IQ 50–55 to 70), which is the largest category (85% of cases), the person can acquire sixth-grade academic skills and can achieve social and vocational skills adequate for self-support.

2. With moderate mental retardation (IQ 35–40 to 50–55), constituting about 10% of cases, the person can achieve only second-grade academic skills but can be vocationally trained for unskilled or semiskilled work under supervision.

3. With severe mental retardation (IQ 20–25 to 35–40), constituting 3%–4% of cases, the person may eventually learn to talk and can be trained in self-care skills but cannot derive much benefit from academic training, although in most cases, the person can live at home or in a closely supervised group home.

4. With profound mental retardation (IQ below 20–25), constituting 1% to 2% of cases, the person usually has considerable impairment in functioning and needs constant supervision and custodial care.

III. *Personality disorders* (PD) have an onset in adolescence or early adulthood; these are relatively permanent and inflexible patterns of interpersonal difficulties and problems with one's sense of self.

A. Someone with a *paranoid PD* distrusts others and is suspicious of people's motives, although there is not a serious break with reality, as in paranoid schizophrenia.

B. Someone with a *schizoid PD* is perceived as cold and uncaring, is detached from social relationships, expresses little emotion, and has no desire to form close relationships.

C. Someone with *schizotypal PD* has peculiar thoughts and speech that interfere with social relationships; these symptoms seem similar to a mild form of schizophrenia.

D. Someone with *antisocial PD* disregards and violates other people's rights and feelings and refuses to follow ethical rules of behavior.

E. Someone with *borderline PD* has marked impulsivity, instability in interpersonal relationships, and sometimes self-destructive behaviors, such as self-mutilation.

F. Someone with *histrionic PD* has excessive emotionality and engages in attention-seeking behaviors, including acting in an infantile manner.

G. Someone with a *narcissistic PD* has a pattern of grandiosity with a need for admiration and lack of empathy.

H. Someone with *avoidant PD* tries to avoid social interaction because of feelings of insecurity and fear of being negatively evaluated.

I. Someone with *dependent PD* needs to be taken care of and develops a submissive and clinging personality.

J. Someone with *obsessive-compulsive PD* shows a preoccupation with orderliness, perfection, and control but does not exhibit true obsessions or compulsive rituals shown by people with obsessive-compulsive disorder.

Essential Reading:

James Butcher, Susan Mineka, and Jill Hooley, *Abnormal Psychology*, 12th ed., chapters 11 and 16.

Supplementary Reading:

American Psychiatric Association, *Diagnostic and Statistical Manual of Mental Disorders*, 4th ed.

Questions to Consider:

1. Some argue that ADHD is over-diagnosed and is actually appropriate evolved behavior, particularly in little boys; in other words, that it was a useful adaptation for getting boys to move around actively in order to learn hunting skills. What do you think about this argument?

2. Many people with personality disorders think that they are perfectly okay; they like their personalities. What criteria should mental health professionals use to distinguish between someone who is a little odd and someone with a true personality disorder?

Lecture Eleven—Transcript
Childhood, Retardation, Personality Disorders

This the last lecture in our series on classifications of mental illness. We have been going through DSM-IV, and we have hit most of the categories so far except for the three that we are going to talk about today. In those three categories, the first one has a rather unwieldy title of disorders usually diagnosed in infancy, childhood, or adolescence. As we will see, it includes a whole lot of things. And then we are going to talk some about mental retardation, a classification that is actually, as you will recall, an Axis-II of the DSM. And then we are going to talk about personality disorders, which is also on the second axis of the DSM. So that is our agenda for today.

Disorders usually diagnosed in infancy, childhood, or adolescence; it is a big category, and it has a lot of things that you may think you would not ever call a mental illness. It has things like stuttering and stammering, communication disorders like that. It has disorders like bedwetting, which is kind of a motor-skills disorder. And you might say to yourself, that those do not sound like mental illnesses to me; and you are right. This is another one of those categories where you need to have them in a classification system so you can get some help. So if your child is having trouble with speaking problems or with math problems or reading problems, you can go get some help and have an insurance company help you with that.

So these disorders include learning, motor skills, and communication disorders. One of the more prominent—I will emphasize three of these subcategories of this classification—and the first one, I am sure all you have heard of, and that is attention-deficit/hyperactivity disorder, sometimes called ADHD. In this case, the child has impulsivity and overactivity that get in the way of completing schoolwork properly, and also in many cases having interpersonal relations that are not good. ADHD occurs in about 5% down to about 3% of school-aged children, depending upon which study you read, and it is six to nine times more prevalent in boys than girls. That is not 6 to 9% more, that is six to nine times the number of boys than girls. Boys are diagnosed with this at a very high rate, especially African-American boys. There is also an ethnicity difference here.

There is some controversy over this, because some people contend that it is over–diagnosed, and that perhaps part of the reason is that we have so many women teachers of boys this age, and they are more used to the way girls behave than the way boys behave. So some people would contend that there is an over-diagnosis of this disorder for boys. It is, if you must admit, that if you look at the way probably our ancestors' kids were brought up, they did not go to school and have to sit in a classroom quietly for six hours a day. They probably ran around in the clearing and played games and did those kinds of things. So we are forcing kids to do something unusual, and there may be a difference in the adaptation for boys than girls; and so that may be part of the reason that ADHD is diagnosed the way it is.

Because of their behavior problems, children with ADHD test from 7 to 15 points lower on average, in terms of IQ tests. And there is some controversy also with respect to whether ADHD continues beyond adolescence. There are people nowadays being diagnosed with adult ADHD, and there are folks who think that might not be a proper diagnosis as well; so there is some controversy there. The most frequently prescribed medication for ADHD is Ritalin, and it is found to be effective in about 75% of the cases. And what is particularly ironic about Ritalin being effective for this when you have a hyperactive kid is that it is a form of amphetamine, which usually brings about more activity; but it does seem to quiet down hyperactive kids. There is some controversy about this in whether there is overmedication for the disorder as well.

Let us move on and talk about autism, which is another category of disorders first diagnosed in infancy, childhood, and adolescence. Autistic children seem to cut themselves off from the world in some respects, and this causes deficits in language, perception, and motor development, as well as difficulties in social situations. Autism occurs in five to seven children out of every 10,000. It is a two to four times more frequent in boys than girls. Autistic children seem to lack the ability to empathize, put themselves in somebody else's place. This often leads to poor social skills. That is what psychologists nowadays are calling "having a theory of mind." Having a theory of mind means that I can figure out as we talk what you are thinking about, and I can respond appropriately and you can do the same with me. We are one of the few animals that can do this.

This is a difference between the primates and us, for example. The primates do not have any theory of mind, and so that is part of the reason why people think that perhaps primates do not have language; that it may be necessary to have a theory of mind to have language. And if autistic children do not have a theory of mind like this, that may explain part of their communication skills, as well as their social skills kinds of problems.

So they often have severe deficits in speech, and they engage in behaviors such as echolalia. Echolalia is if you try to get an autistic child to speak, and you say something to them, like you say, "Say toy," they will say, "Say toy," instead of saying "Toy." They just echo back what you have said as if, again, they do not understand what is in your mind for them to do. All they know to do is echo it back at you. So this parrot-like repeating of phrases is quite common in autistic children. They also engage in self-stimulation, masturbatory behaviors, and also things like spinning and rocking and self-destructive behaviors to some extent, like head banging. Sometimes I have seen autistic children who have to wear boxing gloves to keep them from beating up their face too much and having massive bruises on their face. They will sit there and hit themselves in their face with their fist multiple times, hundreds of times until they are bruising and bleeding from this. It is almost like they are not getting sufficient stimulation from the world, so they have to sort of make up their own stimulation to try to get through to themselves.

Autistic children show large intellectual deficits, but they also sometimes have special, very narrowly defined cognitive abilities— what is sometimes called being a savant—so that they might be particularly good at adding up numbers or something like that, but otherwise they have a strong intellectual deficit. Medications approved are largely ineffective for autism, however, behavior therapies—and we are going to discuss this in a future lecture, what behavior therapies are—but there are programs that have been designed using reinforcement to get children to try to speak, and I will describe some of those when we talk about behavior therapy. They use reinforcement, such as food and drink, and later hugs and kisses to try to get these kids to be able to form speech. Actually, even after they form the speech and they can even speak in sentences, it sounds to us very stilted in their speech. It is sort of like they are trying to imitate somebody, but it is not again coming from deep inside them. So we will talk about that a little bit more.

There is an interesting recent thing that has happened within the last year, to my knowledge at least, and that is the autistic advocacy groups are now arguing that autism is not a mental disorder at all, but that it is an alternative way of being and behaving; much like you hear for advocacy groups for the deaf, who think that it is fine to be deaf, and that they should have their own community and be able to engage in activities with each other, and that it is wrong for the hearing society to force them to have cochlear implants and things like that and learn sign language or learn lip reading. They are okay with sign language but lip reading; they want to be able to consider this to be a deaf community. And much the same way of arguing, these advocacy groups for autism are arguing that maybe we should consider it to be an okay thing to be. It is quite controversial.

Tourette's syndrome you may have heard of. It is a tic disorder where there are muscular contractions that are inappropriate, and sometimes vocal behaviors also. There seems to be, with Tourette's syndrome, a build up of tension that occurs in the person, and that this tension can be relieved by having an outburst of some form or another: a shout or a snort or a yelp or even certain kinds of words. In about a third of the cases, they have what most people associate with Tourette's syndrome, and that is that the words are obscenities.

I was shopping at the grocery store the other day, and was going up the aisle and minding my own business pushing my cart, and I heard right beside me, [sound]. And I turned around and I said, what was that? I thought the woman maybe had a cold or something, and she went shopping along the aisle a little further and then went [sound], like that; and it happened repeatedly. She had Tourette's disorder here. It was a release of this tension that was building up in her. She was controlling it so that she did not shout obscenities. That sometimes happens, and people with Tourette's syndrome with that particular behavior sometimes have a great difficulty, because they will be walking down the street and shout some obscenity out and the person who is passing them will take offense to this, and sometimes get into a fight with them because they think it was meant for them; very strange. If you were writing science fiction and were trying to come up with a mental disorder that seemed to be a very odd thing to have, I think you would invent Tourette's disorder.

But it is not funny to the people who have it, because it is difficult to control; and even after they have certain kinds of therapies to try to control it. You can use some antipsychotic medications that are sometimes effective, and behavior therapies can be effective in terms of decrease in the frequency of the outbursts. But the people would report, even though the frequency of the outbursts has been decreased, they still have this tension; and it is only with great control and concentration that they can overcome the outbursts. So they are not even comfortable very often after the therapy. Tourette's begins around the age of seven, and usually lasts into adulthood.

So those are the disorders of infancy, childhood, and adolescence. Let us move on to the second classification of disorders, and that is mental retardation. And again, let me remind you that we have now moved to Axis-II of the DSM, and that is partly for the reason that a person could have mental retardation and some other clinical syndrome as well from Axis-I.

Mental retardation is the classification for someone who, at less than 18 years of age, has significantly sub-average intelligence and significant limitations in adaptive functioning in at least two areas, such as communication, self-care, academic skills, work, health, and safety. So in order to be classified with this classification under the age of 18—and if it is over the age of 18, you might have a cognitive disorder or something like that—but if it is under the age of 18, you have at least two of those areas problems with it, and a lower IQ score, you would probably be classified as having a form of mental retardation. There are genetic factors that are apparent in mental retardation. It does tend to run in families. And in conditions such as Downs Syndrome, it is particularly prevalent in that case for older mothers and fathers, which is due perhaps to an extra chromosome; that is what the current thinking is in terms of the genetic contribution with Downs Syndrome. It can also be caused by infections or toxic agents that can increase the probability of mental retardation, such as prenatal German measles, and alcohol intoxication during the prenatal period. Also, physical birth traumas such as insufficient oxygen, if the cord gets wrapped around the child's neck and it does not get sufficient oxygen, that can cause a mental retardation. And while it is less frequent today, in the past, radiation, such as exposure to x-rays, was also implicated in mental retardation. We pretty much learned about that sort of thing, so when you go to the dentist today, the dentist will put an apron on you, even if you are a guy, to prevent x-rays from penetrating your body; unlike when I was a kid and we used to go to the shoe store and stick our feet into the x-ray machine while the x-rays were being shot up our legs.

We know a lot more about it now, and so we prevent those kinds of things from happening. Also prenatal dietary deficiencies can cause deficits. So all of these things can cause mental retardation. The degrees of severity of mental retardation, we have names for those degrees of severity, and they are really defined by the intelligent quotient, the measured IQ, of the person. It used to be that we had other names for these kinds of things, and the words idiot, imbecile, and moron, that we use in a derogatory way with each other nowadays were actually once the technical medical names for the various degrees of mental retardation. But when they got these pejorative kinds of meanings to them, that was stopped. Instead they are now called mild retardation, moderate retardation, severe retardation, and profound retardation. So those are the categories, the subcategories, of mental retardation.

Somebody with mild mental retardation has an IQ of somewhere between 50 and 55 up to about 70, and this is the largest category; about 85% of the cases of mental retardation are in this category. And the person with this classification can acquire about 6th grade academic skills, and they can achieve social and vocational skills adequate for self-support. You see these folks out in the community quite often. If you go into a fast-food restaurant and you find somebody working cleaning the tables, or if you go to the supermarket and in the checkout line you may have somebody bagging your groceries who has this classification, and they get along fine in the world under at least fairly controlled kinds of conditions.

Those with moderate mental retardation—that is an IQ of 35–40 in that range up to 50–55, and that is about 10% of the cases of people with the diagnosis of mental retardation—they can achieve only about a 2nd grade academic level in terms of skills, but they can be vocationally trained for unskilled and semiskilled work under supervision. And there are folks who you may run across in thrift stores and that sort of thing who are doing productive work under fairly supervised conditions who might have this classification. I often play my students a tape of a young lady with mild mental retardation, very sweet personality, and she can count forward from one to ten and tries hard to count backwards from ten to one. And she takes things very literally. At one point she has her mouth open, she is yawning, and the fellow doing the interview says, "You have your mouth open, are you sleepy?" And she says, "I always when I am sleepy my mouth is open." And she takes very literally what he is saying. But she is a very sweet and intriguing young lady. If anybody has worked with Special Olympics or something like that, you will find that people with mild and moderate retardation can be a lot of fun to work with.

Severe mental retardation is a category for an IQ level between 20–25 up to 35–40, and this accounts for about 3%–4% of the cases of mental retardation for those who are classified that way. A person in this category can eventually learn to talk, although it is a real struggle; and they can be trained to some extent in self-care skills, but they do not derive much benefit at all from academic training. And the person may be able to live at home if they are closely supervised, or perhaps in a group home.

Profound mental retardation is the most severe form of it, with an IQ of about 20–25. In fact, it begins to be almost impossible to measure IQ at that low a level. And this constitutes about 1% to 2% of the cases of those diagnosed with mental retardation. And this person usually has considerable impairment of functioning and needs constant supervision and custodial care; and most frequently you would find somebody with profound mental retardation in an institutional setting of some sort.

So that is mental retardation, and it is one of the two subcategories under Axis-II. And the other one is personality disorders. Somebody with a personality disorder, it has an onset in adolescence or early adulthood, and these are relatively permanent or inflexible patterns of interpersonal difficulties and problems with one's sense of self. Personality disorders in particular, I think, are going to be difficult for us to deal with. I bet we find a cure for schizophrenia before we find a cure for personality disorders, because it seems to be such a pervasive pattern that a person has, and seems to have less of a hereditary component to it. And people with personality disorders often do not seek any help, because they like their personality. They think they are perfectly all right; it is the rest of us who sometimes have trouble dealing with their personality. So it is a difficult disorder to deal with. There are a number of subcategories of this. Someone could have a paranoid personality; and someone with a paranoid personality—we have already talked about paranoid schizophrenia earlier, so we know what that means—but this would be a person who is suspicious of other people's motives, although there is not a serious break with reality as there is with paranoid schizophrenia. So this person is in touch with reality, they are not having hallucinations; they have these mild delusions that somebody is after them and somebody might be trying to do them harm. Somebody is puncturing their tires on their car or reading their mail or one thing or another that a paranoid personality might think, and that sort of permeates their personality; so they think it is about a lot of people and a lot of situations.

Somebody with a schizoid personality tends to be cold and uncaring; they are detached from social relationships and they express little emotion. They have no desire to form closer relationships either. So if you know somebody who is kind of cold and uncaring and seems to be out for themselves, it could be that they should have a diagnosis of schizoid personality. Somebody with a schizotypal subcategory of a personality disorder has peculiar thoughts and speech that interfere with social relationships. These symptoms are very similar to having schizophrenia, but in a much milder form, and so they may have some of the symptoms that you would usually associate with schizophrenia, but to a far lesser degree.

Someone with antisocial personality disregards other people's rights and violates their rights and refuses to follow ethical rules. So this person just kind of ignores the rules that the rest of us try to live by. Somebody with a borderline personality has marked impulsivity and instability in interpersonal relationships. And sometimes self-destructive behaviors are a part of that, such as self-mutilation; so you find this often in adolescent girls for example, who will cut themselves. And that would be their diagnosis of borderline personality disorder.

The histrionic personality disorder would be somebody who has an excessive emotionality and seeks attention from other people and behaves in an infantile manner. I have a tape that I play my students of a young woman, I think she is 17 or 18, and she had a married boyfriend; got drunk at a union party and spent the night with him, and actually, I guess, she was underage, so he was arrested later. And she is describing this incident and giggling and laughing, much like a young child who is maybe seven or eight years old would be doing. And she is describing this kind of thing and she has a pin cushion that she made that she is sticking needles in and pretending it is the boyfriend and laughing and giggling. And then, right in the middle of the interview, she goes completely the other way, ends up sort of hysterically screaming and yelling and crying and very upset about this guy. Again, much like you would find in a young child who cannot control their emotions and acts in an infantile manner. And while she is only 17, it is likely that this will be a continuing trait. With these personality disorders, these do not tend to come and go, but they are sort of an enduring quality in the personality; and she will probably have at least some of those characteristics as she gets older.

Someone with a narcissistic personality has a pattern of grandiosity with a need for admiration and lack of empathy. So they think they are the best thing that is come along. They do not care much about you; they are all into themselves. They are on what we would sometimes we call an ego trip, although probably, since we now know something about psychoanalysis, they are probably more on an id trip than an ego trip here. So that is narcissistic personality. They are concerned especially about their looks and the way they portray themselves.

Someone with avoidant personality disorder avoids social interaction because of feelings of insecurity and a fear of being negatively evaluated. So this might in fact lead to behavior like agoraphobia that we have already discussed.

Dependent personality needs to be taken care of, so they develop a submissive and clinging personality, and they need somebody else around all the time to try to take care of themselves. And then someone with obsessive-compulsive disorder shows a preoccupation with orderliness, perfection, and control. But this is different from obsessive-compulsive disorder that we talked about earlier in the classification system in that it is not nearly so severe, and they do not have the obsessive thoughts that continually run through their heads, and they do not have the degree of compulsive rituals that they go through about washing their hands many times and that sort of thing. I happen to know a lady with obsessive-compulsive personality and her house is always immaculate; she always has to have everything exactly right in the house, but beyond that she does not exhibit any of the more severe symptoms that you would find in somebody with a truly obsessive-compulsive disorder.

So, what we have done today is go over three of the final categories of mental illness. We have talked about disorders that are diagnosed in infancy, childhood, and adolescence, all the way from the mildest ones like stuttering and stammering up through fairly severe things like autism and Tourette's syndrome. We have talked about mental retardation and what some of the possible causes of mental retardation are and what some of the subcategories are and how we define it based upon IQ. We talked about personality disorders, which are a more permanent part of a person's personality, and talked about the wide variety of different kinds of personalities somebody might have who had that classification.

So this concludes our looking at DSM-IV and the various classifications of the DSM. And so our next step would be, if we are following the medical model, we have now done our diagnosis, and now we want to bring some intervention into effect to try to correct whatever the problem is that we diagnosed. And so that is what we are going to talk about in our next set of lectures, the possible therapies that you can use to intervene to try to correct the problems we have been talking about in this series of lectures. Thank you.

Lecture Twelve
Physical Therapies—Drugs

Scope:

If it is assumed that biology is the primary cause of mental illnesses, then interventions to correct the illnesses should be biological in nature. In particular, if problems exist in biochemistry at the level of the neuron, then a psychopharmacological intervention would seem appropriate. Neurons communicate with one another by means of releasing neurotransmitter substances into the synapses between them. Most drugs work by manipulating the release, reception, or reuptake of neurotransmitters. Antipsychotic drugs have had a major impact on the number of patients in mental hospitals. Traditional antipsychotic drugs are effective but treat only the positive symptoms of psychosis and can have rather severe side effects, such as movement disorders. More recently, use of atypical antipsychotic drugs has become widespread. These drugs treat both negative and positive symptoms and do not have movement side effects. The original MAO-inhibiting and tricyclic antidepressants have been supplanted by selective serotonin reuptake inhibitors, such as Prozac, that are relatively safe and effective. The most widely prescribed antianxiety drugs are tranquilizers, such as Valium, which are quite effective, although sometimes addictive. Naturally occurring lithium and other manufactured drugs are used to control the manic phase of bipolar disorder.

Outline

I. The physical therapies used to correct mental disorders are based on the assumption that the primary causes of the disorders are biological in nature; therefore, interventions ought to be at a physiological level and, in the case of pharmacological interventions, usually at the neuronal level.

    A. Much of human behavior is controlled by neural impulses. Neurons communicate by releasing transmitter substances into the small space between neurons called the *synapse* or *synaptic cleft*.

    B. Packets of neurotransmitter substances are manufactured in the presynaptic neuron and released into the synapse.

C. If there is a proper match, some of the neurotransmitters may be absorbed at receptor sites in the postsynaptic neuron, making that neuron more or less likely to fire.

D. Some of the neurotransmitter substances may also be reabsorbed by the presynaptic neuron in a process called *reuptake.*

E. Many drugs used in psychopharmacological interventions operate by changing the amount of transmitter substance manufactured, by blocking the receptor sites, or by blocking the reuptake of the transmitter substance.

II. Antipsychotic drugs, sometimes also called *neuroleptics* or *major tranquilizers*, are used to treat psychotic disorders associated with schizophrenia or severe mood disorders.

A. These drugs were invented in the mid-1950s and have had a profound effect on the number of patients in mental hospitals and the quality of life of those with psychosis.

B. Of patients treated with traditional antipsychotic drugs, positive symptoms (such as hallucinations and delusions) have been eliminated in approximately 60% of the cases within about 6 weeks, compared with those receiving placebos, 20% of whom have corrected symptoms.

C. Although use of these drugs has reduced the number of patients in institutions, the disorder is not cured, and when patients discontinue using the drugs, they may be repeatedly hospitalized.

D. A major side effect of traditional antipsychotic drugs is movement disorders, the most serious of which is Tardive dyskinesia, a relatively permanent disorder leading to bizarre repetitive movements of the face, tongue, hands, and feet.

E. Within the past decade and a half, atypical antipsychotic drugs have been invented, such as Clozaril, that do not have movement side effects because they are not based on the manipulation of the transmitter substance dopamine, which is also instrumental in movement.

F. These atypical drugs appear to be effective in treating both positive and negative symptoms, such as flattened affect and apathy.

G. Unfortunately, in about 1% of cases, Clozaril can cause a serious side effect called *agranulocytosis*, a drop in white blood cells.

H. However, other variants of atypical drugs do not have this problem; for this reason, atypical drugs are now considered preferable to traditional antipsychotic drugs.

III. The original antidepressant drugs were monoamine oxidase (MAO) inhibitors first used in the 1950s; these inhibit an enzyme in the synapse that helps break down serotonin and norepinephrine.

A. The tricyclic antidepressants have also been around for quite a while; and operate by inhibiting the reuptake of norepinephrine and, to some extent, serotonin.

B. A more effective and less dangerous class of antidepressant drugs was released in 1988, selective serotonin reuptake inhibitors (SSRIs). This class includes the most widely prescribed antidepressant in the world, Prozac.

C. The SSRIs block the reuptake of only serotonin and are much more widely prescribed than the older class of drugs because they have fewer side effects and are not fatal when overdosed.

D. Several other antidepressants are on the market that block both serotonin and norepinephrine (SNRI); others, such as Wellbutrin, are not related to either SSRIs or SNRIs.

E. Although the recent generations of antidepressants are quite effective, they are sometimes prescribed inappropriately for those without serious depressive disorders, and there are some data indicating a link to teenage suicide.

IV. The original antianxiety drugs were the barbiturates, but because of dangers associated with them, these are seldom used today except to control seizures.

A. In the 1960s, tranquilizers, technically known as *benzodiazepines*, became the drugs most widely prescribed for anxiety symptoms.

B. These drugs, such as Valium, are quite effective at lower doses in relieving anxiety symptoms and at higher doses in sedating patients.

C. Although generally considered safe, tranquilizers can be addictive and can cause withdrawal symptoms.

V. Lithium and some other drugs can be used to control the manic phase of bipolar disorder.

A. Lithium was discovered in the 1940s in Australia but was not used in the United States until 1970.

B. It is unclear why lithium works to control mood; although it is effective in many cases (70% to 80% of cases show improvement), it can be highly toxic and dosages must be carefully monitored.

C. Several other newer drugs can now be used in treating bipolar disorder in addition to lithium.

Essential Reading:

James Butcher, Susan Mineka, and Jill Hooley, *Abnormal Psychology*, 12th ed., chapter 17.

Supplementary Reading:

Peter Nathan and J. M. Gorman, eds., *A Guide to Treatments That Work*.

Questions to Consider:

1. Given that none of the drugs mentioned in this lecture can cure mental illness (they all just treat symptoms), what kind of therapy do you think it will take to actually provide a cure?

2. Most psychologists think that mental illnesses are caused by the interplay of our biology with our life experiences. If this is the case, how likely do you think it is that we can effectively treat mental illnesses solely using biological interventions (drugs)?

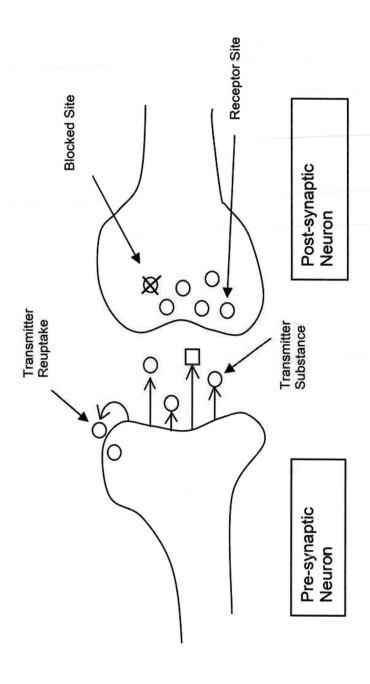

Blocked Site

Receptor Site

Post-synaptic Neuron

Transmitter Reuptake

Transmitter Substance

Pre-synaptic Neuron

Lecture Twelve—Transcript
Physical Therapies—Drugs

In this lecture we are going to start a series where we are talking about therapies. Where we have just been, as we have talked about the classification system for mental illnesses and following a medical model, once you do diagnosis then you should be doing a therapy to try to correct whatever problem that you have diagnosed. That seems quite logical. In a medical model, the logic is clearer, where there is a specific therapy for a specific disorder. As we will discover when we are talking about therapies here, that which therapy you pick kind of depends upon what you think about the disease. And as we have been going through these mental disorders, we have noticed that there has been some controversy over the causes of the disease. When you have a controversy over the causes of the disease, then you have a controversy over how you ought to intervene to correct whatever the problem is. Again, in a medical model, if you have a problem with appendicitis, the cause is pretty obvious, what that problem is. But if you have a problem with depression, is the root cause biological in nature? Is it something you had inherited in your genes? Is it something that is bad about your biochemistry, of your body? Or is it something that is happening in your life that is causing you to be depressed? Or is it having learned inappropriate kinds of responses to things in your life? And depending upon your answer to that question, you might want to intervene at a different level.

So that is why there are a number of therapies and why I am grouping these therapies as I am. Today, we are going to start talking about physical therapies; and in particular today we are going to talk about psychopharmacological intervention, the use of drugs. And the starting assumption there is that we have a physiological problem here; it is a brain problem, at least a central nervous system problem, and if you are going to intervene, you have to intervene at that level. So we are going to talk some about neurons and the effects of transmitter substances and that sort of thing today. But you can also intervene at a physical level in other ways.

In future lectures, we are going to talk about electroconvulsive shock treatment, which is certainly another physical way of intervening. We are going to talk some about psychosurgery, actually going in and changing the structure of the brain. And we are also going to talk at least about the future possibilities of gene therapy. And those are all kinds of physical interventions as well.

Following that, we are going to talk about the talking therapies, psychoanalysis and cognitive therapies and the humanistic therapies that are involved in trying to talk to somebody. And you would use a talking therapy if you believe that the problems are caused by the way people are thinking about things. That is what Freud thought— at the unconscious level there was this thought and this great amount of conflict, and so if you are going to intervene, you do not intervene by changing the neurotransmitter substance; you intervene by getting people to think about things in a different way. So you talk to them about this. So that is the general notion with the talking therapies.

Finally, there is a set of therapies called behavior therapies, which are based upon the general notion that people have learned inappropriate responses to things. And behavior therapies are based on simple learning, like classical conditioning. And so we will talk about those therapies based on the simple, classical conditioning model. And we will also talk about those therapies based upon operant conditioning. So that is where we're going to go in the next set of lectures, is talking about these various therapies.

Today then we are going to begin by considering physical therapies, and in particular, drugs. Human behavior is really controlled at the neural level, through neural impulses. We are made up of nerves, of course, that go all over our body. And in those nerves we have neurons, and they are packed with these neurons; and if somebody touches our skin, in fact, a message is sent through these neurons up the nerves to our central nervous system, to the spine first and then to the brain, and then various components of the brain talk to each other through these neurons and eventually send messages back down to our muscles to tell us how to behave given the processing that the brain did. And all of that is being done by the neurons.

We are packed with millions of neurons in our central nervous system, and these neurons have to communicate with one another. Now we could have a whole course, and we could talk about how the neural impulse travels along the neuron, but what I want to be concerned about in particular is how a single neuron talks to another single neuron. The way they do this is by having an upstream neuron—what I will call a pre-synaptic neuron, prior to the synapse.

The synapse is the space between neurons, it is kind of a small gap; and then you have a post-synaptic neuron. So if you will picture on one side having a pre-synaptic neuron, and then a bit of a space, and then a post-synaptic neuron. What happens when these neurons talk to one another, when the upstream, the presynaptic neuron, has just fired, the next thing that is likely to happen is that it will release some transmitter substance, a chemical, into this gap, into this synapse. That chemical can cross the gap and have various effects on the downstream neuron, the post-synaptic neuron, and it can release various kinds of transmitter substances. There are different neurons that release different transmitter substances, and there may be multiple neurons dumping these transmitter substances into the synapse and different transmitter substances. And then whether those transmitter substances are having an effect is dependent upon the downstream, the post-synaptic neuron. The post-synaptic neuron has certain receptors in it. In much like a key fits into a lock, these receptors are responsive to only certain of the transmitter substances that have been released into the synaptic cleft, or into the synapse.

So you have the upstream neuron releasing transmitter substances, crosses the synapse and looks for a sites—I am getting a little anthropomorphic here—but it does not have its own intelligence, of course; but in fact it bathes the downstream neuron. And the transmitter substance will fit into certain sites there. If it does fit into certain sites, it makes that next neuron more likely to fire or, in some cases, less likely to fire. It depends upon whether it is exciting or inhibiting the next neuron. And so that is the basic anatomy of how one neuron communicates with another neuron. Now we have to be a little bit more specific about this.

The upstream neuron, when it releases this transmitter substance, it can or cannot affect the downstream neuron, depending upon certain kinds of things. It is possible that some of those sites where the neurotransmitter substance could fit in have been blocked in some way, and that is one of the actions that you can have with drugs, is to block the downstream sites so that transmitter cannot fit into the keyhole; the keyhole already has a key in it, and will not allow this transmitter substance to fit in. That is one way that you could affect behavior.

Another way that could affect behavior with a drug is to get it to release more of the transmitter substance from the upstream neuron, from the pre-synaptic neuron. It could release more transmitter substance, in which case it might fight into more sites on the post-synaptic neuron and make it more likely to fire or even less likely to fire, depending upon how many sites it could fit in. So how much transmitter substances being released you can affect with drugs as well.

These transmitter substances, when they are released into the gap there, not all of them are used, not all of them fit into sites; and for what is left over, there is a process called "reuptake," whereby they are reabsorbed into the upstream neuron. So it has released it, it has affected some of the sites, there is some left over, and it is reabsorbed into the neuron. Again, drugs can affect the reabsorption process and keep it from being reabsorbed quite as quickly, in which case there is more of the transmitter substance still sitting in the synapse that might affect the downstream neuron.

So those are just some of the ways that drugs affect neural transmission. So we will be talking about drugs and referring to things like a reuptake inhibitor. What that means is that it inhibits the reabsorption of that neurotransmitter substance from the pre-synaptic neuron. So that is a brief crash course in neural transmission, and that tells us a little bit about what we might be able to do using drugs to try to affect people's behavior. And these drugs usually have their effects on the communication that is being done using transmitter substances. There are some drugs that are a bit different, that affect hormones and other kinds of things, but for the most part, the drugs we are talking about will be having their effect on the transmitter substance.

Now I have oversimplified by a huge amount what I just talked about. I am pretending there is one upstream neuron and there is one downstream neuron and there is one synapse. When in fact what you typically have, if you could actually take a picture of what is going on, it is possible to do that nowadays and if they take a picture there are many upstream neurons and many downstream neurons and the synaptic clefts are all sort of pushed together and there is all sorts of different kinds of transmitter substances some having excitatory effects and firing off the downstream neurons, some having inhibitory affects, some counteracting each other in the synapse, some having reuptake and some not having reuptake, it is a very complex kind of thing as you can imagine if you have millions and millions of these neurons in your central nervous system.

So I have oversimplified by a great margin, and sometimes when we have drugs that affect these things, we are not quite sure of what is going on here. The drug companies, I hate to admit it, but sometimes what they do is mess around with drugs that they know work, and do a slight tweak of the chemistry of the drug and try it again, never being quite sure what is going on in terms of the transmitter substances and exactly what the effect is of that particular drug. It is only been in recent years we have known the effects of many of the drugs that the drug companies produce. So it is a complex situation and we will only be able to get a glimmer of what goes on with these kinds of drugs.

What I would next like to do is move on and talk about some of the drugs that we do use in therapies, and the effects of some of those kinds of drugs. And I hope we keep in mind what we just learned about neurotransmitter substance and the communications of neurons with one another as we talk about these.

One class of drugs, a very important class of drugs, is the antipsychotic drugs. These are sometimes called neuroleptics; that is their technical name. They have also, in the past, been called major tranquilizers, although that is a bit of a misnomer, and we probably should not call them that. But if you ever hear of anybody talking about those, they are probably talking about the antipsychotic drugs. These are used to treat psychotic disorders such as schizophrenia or severe mood disorders. We talked about, in the manic phase of bipolar disorder, antipsychotic drugs are sometimes used.

These drugs were invented in the mid-1950s, and they had a profound effect upon the number of people who are in mental hospitals, and also the general characteristics of a mental institution. If you look at the number of people in mental institutions, over the years, you will see an increasing number. Between the mid-1950s and 1960, there was a marked change in that, and the ever-upward trend turned into to a downward trend; and the major reason for that were the antipsychotic drugs, especially the antipsychotic drugs and their effect on schizophrenic patients, who then began to be able to leave the hospital. So that was one of the major contributors to the fact that our mental hospitals have fewer people in it today than you would expect.

There were some other contributors, and I think we will talk a little bit about those as the course goes on; contributors such as the ability to sue doctors, and the ability to ensure through the legal system that you are getting treatment in mental institutions, and that sort of thing. There are actually far fewer people in mental institutions today than one would predict. If you take the 1955 figures in fact, in mental institutions where there are about—I believe there are about 900,000 people in mental institutions today—if you extrapolated the population in the country today and the proportion of people who are in mental institutions in 1955, we would have almost a million. We have about 70,000 in mental institutions today. One of the major reasons is the antipsychotic drugs, and also some court rulings and some other kinds of things that have affected that.

It also changed the way mental institutions are. If you visit a mental institution today, you will find it quite quiet. You will see people sitting around and maybe rocking and maybe doing some strange things, but for the most part you do not see people screaming and yelling and running around and kind of out of control. The major reason is the antipsychotic drugs. Prior to the antipsychotic drugs, mental institutions were bedlam. That is kind of an inside joke, because bedlam is the name of a mental institution; that is where that name came from. And it was kind of a mess; and the drugs, because they attack the positive symptoms of psychosis, and in particular schizophrenia, they quiet the patients down markedly.

Of patients who are treated with traditional antipsychotic drugs, the positive symptoms, the hallucinations, delusions, and so forth, have been eliminated in approximately 60% of the cases within about 6 weeks compared to those receiving placebos that have only 20% reduction in those positive symptoms. And so that is a pretty good result. Now, perhaps not as good as what you might think, because they are not cured. In fact, none of the therapies I am going to talk about, of the ones currently in use, cure anybody. When we get to the gene therapies and start talking about the possibility for the future, there may be the possibility of a cure, but right now the kinds of therapies we use do not cure the person. They, for the most part, just get rid of the symptoms. And so a person taking antipsychotic drugs should continue to take the antipsychotic drugs. And one of the problems that we have nowadays is that somebody gets diagnosed with schizophrenia; let us say, they are acting oddly, their family is afraid, they checked them into the psychiatric hospital, and they are evaluated and it is determined that indeed they have a diagnosis of schizophrenia. They go before a hearing in the legal system, have a lawyer to argue their case, but their behavior is indeed bizarre and they end up in a mental institution. They usually, in that case, if they are diagnosed as schizophrenic, they would start them on these antipsychotic drugs, and the drugs would begin to take effect. And over a six-week period of time, maybe several months, their behavior, at least the positive symptoms decrease; they look like they are getting better and better. And maybe after a six-month period of time or a year's period of time, they come up for reevaluation by the institution and the legal system, and they let them loose. They get on a bus and go home.

Now, we hope that there is some community health interventions going on where they might pick them up and make sure they try to take the drug, but most people do not like taking these drugs. There are some negative side effects I am about to talk about, and they do not go well with alcohol, and there are some other kinds of problems where they do not like to take the drug. So quite typically, they will quit taking the drug; six months later they are displaying the symptoms again. They are recommitted, they are sent back to the mental institution. They are there for another six months to a year, they are on the drugs, they get let out they go home again, they quit taking the drugs; and there is this cycle where they are cycling in and out of the institution. It is good news that we have fewer people in mental institutions, but it is kind of bad news that we don't have a way of supporting the folks who are getting out of the institutions better than we do so that we keep them on the drugs.

A major side effect of traditional antipsychotic drugs is a movement disorder, or several kinds of movement disorders, the most serious of which is Tardive dyskinesia. Tardive dyskinesia is a relatively permanent disorder that affects the movements of the face, tongue, hands, and feet. I remember the first time I saw somebody with this; it was back about the time that these drugs were first being used, and this fellow, who had just gotten out of the institution—he was a relative of a neighbor and he was visiting and it scared me to death. I was fairly young at the time. I have never seen somebody like this. And he would have these extreme grimaces on his face, where his mouth would open up and he would have this, sort of frightening—to a kid at least—look on his face; and he could not control it. It was a major side effect. At that point they were still trying to figure out how much of these drugs to give people, and the problem is that these typical drugs work on dopamine as the neurotransmitter substance—that is the substance being released into the synapse—and somehow they are having a good effect on the positive symptoms of schizophrenia. But dopamine is also one of the major transmitter substances that controls movement for us; and so it is not surprising that, if you are messing around with the dopamine in the synapse, that you get movement disorders of one form or another. Not everybody gets these disorders, but a large enough proportion of people do that it is a real problem. And the disorders, once they get fairly severe, often do not go away.

Within the past decade and a half, a new kind of antipsychotic drug has been invented called an atypical antipsychotic drug; the first one of those was Clozaril. I am not sure whether you have heard of Clozaril. It is a particularly effective drug; it seems to get rid of the positive symptoms, and it also seems to have some effect on the negative symptoms, which the traditional antipsychotic drugs did not have. So it is good in that way, and it is also good in that it does not, because it does not work on the dopamine system—it does not have these negative movement side effects like Tardive dyskinesia either. Unfortunately, it does have one bad symptom, and that is that there is a problem with red blood cells that is affected by Clozaril; and because of that—it is called agranulocytosis—and there is a drop in white blood cells. And we need our white blood cells, because they fight infection. It only occurs in about 1% of the cases, but it is kind of a deadly thing that happens when it occurs. And for this reason, people on Clozaril end up having to have a lot of blood tests to make sure that they are not getting agranulocytosis; and insurance companies in particular do not like that, because they end up spending $45,000 a year on blood tests for these folks. And so that influences to some degree what kinds of medications are prescribed.

Fortunately, there are some other atypical antipsychotic drugs that have been invented that do not have this side effect of agranulocytosis; and the drug companies are very active in looking for new atypical kinds of drugs, and I think there is a great hope for that for the future.

Let us move on now and talk about antidepressant drugs. There is kind of an old-fashioned version of antidepressant drugs that were first used in the 1950s called monoamine oxidase inhibitors, or, for short, MAOs. These inhibit an enzyme in the synapse that helps break down serotonin and norepinephrine—those are two more transmitter substances that are having their effect in the synapse. So there is an enzyme there that breaks down these two transmitter substances. There are also tricyclic antidepressants; they have around for a while also, and they operate by inhibiting the re-uptake of both norepinephrine and, to some extent, serotonin. They are still used to some degree, but a lot of these earlier kinds of drugs, the antidepressant drugs, have been replaced by what are called selective serotonin re-uptake inhibitors. So, in fact, what that means basically is serotonin, which is being dumped into the synapse, you inhibit the re-uptake; and so there is more serotonin left in the synapse to affect the downstream neuron. So that is how they have their effect. These are sometimes called SSRIs, and they are exemplified by the drug that was released in 1988 called Prozac. I am sure everybody has heard of Prozac. Lots of folks take Prozac. There are other drugs like Paxil and Zoloft that are also used, but Prozac fairly quickly became one of the biggest selling drugs that exist. These SSRIs block the reuptake of only serotonin, and for that reason they are more widely prescribed, and they have fewer side effects. And one good thing is that they are also not fatal when they are overdosed, the way the earlier drugs were. There are several other antidepressants that are on the market that block both serotonin and norepinephrine, and these are sometimes called SNRIs. And there are others, such as Wellbutrin, that are really not related to either of those things.

While the recent generation of antidepressants are quite effective, they are sometimes prescribed inappropriately for those without serious depressive disorders; and in fact for a while there was the fear that people were taking these things just to feel better when they were perfectly normal and did not have any problems. There is also a problem with a possible link to teenage suicide and perhaps even adult suicide. It has been known for some time that there may be a darker side to these drugs in terms of suicide. There was an article that was just published earlier this year in which adults—it was found that adults taking one of these antidepressant drugs or one of the several available antidepressant drugs were twice as likely to attempt suicide as adults on a placebo, on a sugar placebo. And partly for that reason, recently it has been required to put a label on the side of these, although the label is pretty much pointed at more youthful users. But it is probably true for adults that people ought to be watched very closely, because of the possibility of suicide.

Now before we get too excited about that, we should understand that, at least for severe problems with depression, it is safer to put a person on the drug than not, particularly if you watch them. And the actual incidence of successful suicides has dropped since these drugs came into effect. The real message is probably that we should not use these drugs and mis-prescribe them for rather mild conditions. We ought to be using them for what they were designed for, and that is for major depression; when there in fact is a threat of suicide to begin with. Part of what may be going on with the suicide is that you have this person who is so depressed that they have been unable to accomplish almost anything, including suicide, because they cannot just get up the energy to even do anything. Then you put them on the antipsychotic drug and they are suddenly released enough that they are able to do something; and one of things—they are still not at the point where they have gotten rid of those suicidal thoughts, and they may go ahead and try to commit suicide at that point. That is why, especially when they start on the drug, they need to be carefully watched.

Let me move on to talk for just a minute about the anti-anxiety drugs. Originally barbiturates were used for antianxiety purposes, but they are quite dangerous as a class of drugs, and they are seldom used today except to control seizures. In the 1960s, tranquilizers came into being; these are called benzodiazepines, that is the technical name for them, although we know them as things like Valium and Milltown and that sort of thing. These are the most widely prescribed for anxiety symptoms, and they are particularly effective in lower doses. Lots of people take these drugs. We know that anxiety, from looking at the classification systems, is one of the major classes of mental disorders, so it is not surprising that there are many, many prescriptions written for these. And in general they are fairly safe when taken at a prescribed level. When they are over-prescribed or overtaken, they can be addictive and cause withdrawal symptoms.

Finally, let me just talk a minute about Lithium. For the manic phase of bipolar disorder, Lithium is sometimes used. Lithium was discovered in the 1940s in Australia, but it was not widely used in the U.S. until about 1970, probably because nobody can make much money off of Lithium. It is kind of a naturally occurring chemical; nobody can patent it; it is there. So, partly for this reason, it did not get a lot of marketing until about 1970. It is unclear why Lithium works to control mood, but it is very effective in cases—and in about 70-80% of cases, people show improvement for their manic phase of bipolar disorder. However, it also can be highly toxic, and the dosage must be carefully monitored. A good deal of what happens early on in bipolar disorder is trying to establish the levels of medication, and the tradeoff of the antidepressive drugs, with the antimanic drugs, such as Lithium. And there are some newer drugs being used for the mania phase of bipolar disorder as well.

So today, we have had a quick, little tutorial on the workings of neurons and how they talk to one another, and the effects of transmitter substances. And then we have gone over several different kinds of drugs, the antipsychotics, the antidepressants, the antianxiety drugs; and looked at some of their effects and how neurotransmitter substances used for these particular kinds of drugs. Thank you.

Timeline

1662 ....René Descartes publishes *Treatise on Man*, proposing a mind-body dualism.

1690 ....John Locke publishes *Essay Concerning Human Understanding*, stating, "There is nothing in the mind that was not first in the senses."

1739 ....David Hume publishes *A Treatise of Human Nature*, claiming that the mind is a collection of sensory impressions linked by associations.

1834 ....Ernst Weber publishes *On Touch: Anatomical and Physiological Notes*, demonstrating the quantification of mental operations.

1871 ....Charles Darwin publishes *The Descent of Man*, applying evolutionary theory to humans.

1879 ....Wilhelm Wundt establishes the first psychological laboratory in Leipzig, Germany.

1890 ....William James publishes *The Principles of Psychology*, introducing the empirical science of psychology to America.

1900 ....Sigmund Freud publishes *The Interpretation of Dreams*, his first major work on psychoanalytic theory.

c. 1906 ....Ivan Pavlov discovers classical conditioning, although *Conditioned Reflexes: An Investigation of the Physiological Activity of the*

Cerebral Cortex was not published until 1927.

1913 ....John Watson publishes an article in *Psychological Review* introducing the concepts of behaviorist psychology.

1950 ....B. F. Skinner publishes a paper titled "Are theories of learning necessary?" arguing that psychology should build its science only on observable behaviors.

1967 ....Ulric Neisser publishes *Cognitive Psychology*, arguing that mental operations can be studied scientifically.

1975 ....Edward O. Wilson publishes *Sociobiology: The New Synthesis*, claiming that modern evolutionary theory can explain much of human behavior.

Glossary

Alzheimer's disease: A cognitive disorder usually associated with older adults, characterized by progressive deterioration of cognitive functions, particularly memory.

Anal stage: In psychoanalytic theory, the developmental stage in which psychosexual energy is focused on the anus and anal activities, such as toilet training.

Antipsychotic drugs: A category of psychopharmacological intervention used to alleviate the symptoms of psychosis; this classification includes both traditional drugs that treat positive symptoms and atypical drugs that treat negative symptoms and have fewer undesirable side effects.

Anxiety disorders: The classification of mental disorders, formerly called *neuroses*, in which the major symptom is apprehension of possible danger.

Autism: A mental disorder that begins in childhood and is characterized by a disconnect from the social world, problems with social skills and speech, and self-stimulation.

Avoidance learning: A type of learning in which a stimulus that is paired with an aversive event signals the organism, which can then behave in a way to avoid the aversive event.

Behavior therapies: A classification of therapies based on the assumption that inappropriate classical or operant conditioning has taken place, in which the goal of therapy is to set up the conditions for appropriate re-learning to occur.

Behaviorism: A school of thought in psychology having its major influence from the early 1900s through about 1970, in which the mind was ignored and only behavior was considered the appropriate subject matter.

Biofeedback: A behavior therapy in which operant conditioning is used to condition a biological response normally considered to be involuntary.

Bipolar depression: A classification of mental disorders characterized by mood swings between depression and mania.

Cannon-Bard theory: A theory of emotion proposing that a stimulus causes a change in activation of the thalamus in the brain that then simultaneously sends messages to the cortex, interpreted as emotion, and to the physiological systems.

Classical conditioning: A type of basic learning discovered by Ivan Pavlov; an unconditioned stimulus, which automatically brings about an unconditioned response, is repeatedly paired with a conditioned stimulus until the conditioned stimulus comes to evoke a conditioned response.

Cognitive disorder: A classification of mental disorders that results from brain impairments leading to disturbances of consciousness or deficits in cognition or memory.

Cognitive-labeling theory: A theory of emotion proposed by Stanley Schachter, proposing that a stimulus causes generalized physiological activation, which then, depending on the context, is labeled as a particular emotion.

Cognitive psychology: A school of thought in psychology having its major influence beginning in the late 1960s through today, in which it is considered appropriate to use various methods to determine the flow of information and processing stages in the brain.

Cognitive therapy: A classification of therapies based on the goal of helping clients understand their thoughts and feelings so that they can reprogram these to achieve greater happiness and success.

Concept formation: A type of learning in which the individual must learn the defining dimensions of a concept by experiencing instances that confirm or disconfirm that concept.

Confounding variable: In an experiment, a circumstance with levels that are correlated with the levels of the independent variable, such that any change in the dependent variable could be due either to changes in the independent variable or changes in the confounding variable.

Consolidation theory: A theory of forgetting that proposes that time is required for memory traces to consolidate, that is, to become permanent enough that they cannot be interfered with by other salient events.

Control variable: In an experiment, a circumstance set by the experimenter at a particular level and not allowed to vary.

Correlational observation: A research method in which the statistical relationship between two or more variables can be determined, but the causality of this relationship cannot be determined.

Decay theory: A theory of memory that attributes memory loss to the fading of a memory trace as a result of the passage of time.

Depressant: A psychoactive drug that has a calming effect on the user.

Developmental psychology: The branch of psychology concerned with studying behavior across the lifespan.

Diagnostic and Statistical Manual of Mental Disorders: A document published by the American Psychiatric Association that classifies the various mental disorders.

Differential parental investment: In evolutionary theory, the concept that women have a much higher investment in their offspring, because of gestation, lactation, and so on, than do men.

Dissociative disorders: A classification of mental disorders in which some parts of the self become separated from the other parts.

Ego: In psychoanalytic theory, the part of the personality that operates on a reality principle and tries to determine what an individual should realistically do while still trying to satisfy the id and the superego.

Electroconvulsive shock treatment: A physical therapy, sometimes called ECT, in which electrical current is passed through the brain; usually used to treat symptoms of depression.

Engineering psychology: A branch of psychology that is concerned with specifying the characteristics and limitations of the human operator in a human-machine-environment system.

Ergonomics: An interdisciplinary field, also sometimes called *human factors*, concerned with the design of human-machine-environment systems.

Evolutionary theory: A scientific theory first proposed by Charles Darwin in the 1800s that uses the idea of survival of the fittest to explain the wide diversity of plants and animals in the world.

Experiment: A scientific method in which an independent variable is manipulated and a dependent variable is measured while other possible variables are accounted for such that it is possible to infer causality.

Gestalt school: A German school of perceptual thought that proposes that we have certain built-in principles, such as proximity, similarity, closure, and good figure, by which we organize parts of perceptual events into wholes.

Genital stage: In psychoanalytic theory, the final developmental stage, in which a truly intimate, sharing, and caring relationship can develop.

Hamilton's rule: A formula in evolutionary theory, $c < r \times b$, that attempts to explain altruism; according to the formula, we should act if the cost to us (c) is less than our relatedness to the person we are helping (r) times the benefit (b) to the person we are helping.

Homeostatic model: A biologically based theory of motivation in which the organism has a need that leads to a drive; the drive, in turn, leads to behavior that returns the organism to an optimal state.

Humanistic therapies: A classification of therapies, such as non-directive and existential, in which the goal is to improve the client's understanding of thoughts and feelings so that the client can achieve his or her full potential.

Id: In psychoanalytic theory, the part of the personality that operates on a pleasure principle; if unchecked by the superego or ego, the id would drive us to take whatever we wanted, whenever we wanted it.

Illusory memories: Under certain conditions, people will recall events that did not actually occur; this indicates that memory is a constructive process, in which memory cues are used in an attempt to reconstruct the original memory.

Inclusive fitness: A concept in evolutionary theory proposing that organisms behave in ways that improve the chances that all kin, not just children, will survive and reproduce.

Independent variable: In an experiment, the circumstance chosen by the experimenter to manipulate in order to determine its effects on the dependent variable.

Interference theory: A theory of memory that attributes memory loss to interfering material that occurs either before or after the event to be remembered.

Introspection: A technique in early experimental psychology in which trained observers attempted to analyze the contents of their own minds by reflecting on their thoughts and perceptions.

James-Lange theory: A theory of emotion proposing that a stimulus causes both a behavioral and a physiological reaction, and it is the latter that leads to an emotional feeling.

Mental retardation: A classification of mental disorder characterized by significantly subaverage intelligence and limitations on functioning.

Mnemonics: Aids used to improve memory.

Mood disorders: The classification of mental disorders in which there is an uncontrollable, undesirable change in emotion, such as unipolar or bipolar depression.

Narcotic: A psychoactive drug usually derived from the opium plant that gives the user a rush and is highly physiologically addictive.

Non-directive therapy: A type of humanistic therapy (also sometimes called *client-centered*), in which the therapist tries to act as a mirror to reflect the clients' thoughts and feelings so that clients gain the ability to solve their own problems.

Oedipus conflict: In psychoanalytic theory, the conflict that develops during the phallic stage when little boys unconsciously want to sexually possess their mothers but find their fathers in the way.

Operant conditioning: A type of simple learning, also sometimes called *instrumental conditioning*, in which a response is more likely to recur if followed by a reinforcement.

Oral stage: In psychoanalytic theory, the first developmental stage and the stage in which psychosexual energy is focused on the mouth.

Perceptual constancies: A school of perception proposing that early in life, we learn that certain properties of objects are invariant, such as size, shape, brightness, and color.

Perceptual illusions: Situations in which our internal perceptual model of the external world is not in correspondence with reality, causing us to make mistakes in what we perceive.

Phallic stage: In psychoanalytic theory, the developmental stage especially important for little boys, in which psychosexual energy is focused on the penis and aggressive competition begins.

Phobia: A classification of mental disorders in which there is an undue fear of objects or situations.

Polygraph: A machine, also called a *lie detector*, that measures heart rate, blood volume, breathing rate, and galvanic skin response in an attempt to determine whether a person is being truthful.

Population stereotypes: The expectations that users of human-machine-environment systems have about the effect of their actions.

Prefrontal lobotomy: A surgical technique in which the connections between the prefrontal cortex and the rest of the brain are severed; this technique was used for several decades in the middle of the 20th century to alleviate the symptoms of long-term schizophrenic patients.

Probability learning: A type of learning in which the individual learns the underlying probabilistic structure of the environment.

Psychoanalysis: A psychotherapy developed primarily by Sigmund Freud, based on psychoanalytic theory, in which the goal is an analysis of the unconscious.

Psychoanalytic theory: A theory of personality proposed by Sigmund Freud in the early 1900s, in which the unconscious plays a major role in determining behavior and the parts of the personality, the id, superego, and ego, are in constant conflict.

Psychosis: Mental disorders that are characterized by a break with reality.

Qualitative design: A research design, such as ethnography, in which patterns of behavior can be studied, but these observations are not amiable to quantitative analysis.

Random variable: In an experiment, a circumstance allowed to vary in a random way such that it is uncorrelated with the levels of the independent variable.

Schizophrenia: A classification of mental disorders in which there is a psychotic break with reality and often delusions, hallucinations, and disorganized speech and behaviors.

Self-actualization: A goal proposed by Abraham Maslow in his Hierarchy of Needs model of motivation, in which people can fulfill their full potential.

Sexual disorders: A classification of mental disorders in which there is either an inability to perform sexually as desired or sexual behavior characterized by an undue sexual attraction to abnormal sexual stimuli.

Social psychology: A branch of psychology concerned with social thinking, social influence, and social relations.

Somatoform disorder: A classification of mental disorders in which there are complaints about bodily symptoms or defects.

Stimulant: A psychoactive drug that produces feelings of heightened awareness and alertness.

Stimulus discrimination: In classical conditioning, when stimulus generalization has occurred, if similar stimuli continue to be presented, but only the conditioned stimulus is paired with the unconditioned stimulus, the responses to the similar stimuli will die out.

Stimulus generalization: In classical conditioning, after acquisition takes place and the conditioned stimulus reliably evokes the conditioned response, other similar stimuli also are found to evoke some lesser level of response.

Substance-related disorder: A classification of mental disorders related to problems caused by taking a drug of abuse.

Superego: In psychoanalytic theory, the part of the personality that operates on a moral principle much like our conscience and gives us guilt when we do not follow its rules.

Systematic desensitization: A behavior therapy in which clients pair up progressively more anxiety-producing situations with relaxation in order to learn new, more appropriate responses to these situations.

Token economy: In behavior therapies based on operant conditioning, when a symbolic reinforcer is used, such as a poker chip, that can be traded for a primary reinforcer, such as food.

Tourette's syndrome: A mental disorder characterized by a continuous repeated build-up of tension that sometimes leads to uncontrollable vocal and motor outbursts.

Transmitter substance: A chemical released into the synapse between neurons that makes the postsynaptic neuron more or less likely to fire.

Unconscious level: In psychoanalytic theory, the part of the personality below the level of awareness that plays a major role in determining how we behave.

Unipolar depression: A classification of mental disorders characterized by either depressed mood or loss of interest in pleasurable activities.

Biographical Notes

Charles Darwin (1809–1882). A British naturalist who, after his 1831–1836 trip collecting plant and animal specimens, wrote the classic book *On the Origin of Species*, published in 1859. This book was the basis for the theory of evolution, including the concept of natural selection and the theory's requirements of variation, inheritance, and selection. Later, Darwin would add the concept of sexual selection to his theory and would apply the theory to humans.

Sigmund Freud (1856–1939). An Austrian physician who, while treating patients with hysteria (conversion disorder) using hypnotism, discovered that patients improved if he could get them to talk about their problems. Over the years, he developed this therapeutic technique into psychoanalysis and proposed the associated psychoanalytic theory. This theory's emphasis on the unconscious level is the basis of many modern-day social policies, as well as today's psychodynamic therapies.

William James (1842–1910). An American psychologist who, with his 1890 textbook *The Principles of Psychology*, introduced scientific psychology to many university students and faculty. Although he was not a researcher, he was an outstanding philosopher and writer, well versed in psychological findings from around the world. He was adept at combining his knowledge of psychology with his personal observations to bring psychology alive to his readers.

Ivan Petrovitch Pavlov (1849–1936). A Russian physiologist who won the Nobel Prize for his research into the physiology of digestion; in the course of his research, he observed that pairings of certain events led to responses to new stimuli. From these observations and later experimentation, he founded the field of classical conditioning. Although he spent the rest of his career studying conditioned reflexes, he denied to the end that he was a psychologist.

Burrhus Frederic (B. F.) Skinner (1904–1990). An American psychologist who many consider to be the father of operant conditioning; his first major book, *The Behavior of Organisms*, was published in 1938. He also wrote *Walden Two*, a fictional treatment of a utopian society based on reinforcement, and *Beyond Freedom and Dignity*, a book considering the uses of reinforcement for social engineering. Skinner's early work on schedules of reinforcement formed the basis for modern behavior therapies.

John Broadus Watson (1879–1958). An American psychologist who became uncomfortable with introspection as a research technique and, following Pavlov's lead, founded the school of psychology known as behaviorism, which he introduced in a 1913 article entitled "Psychology as the Behaviorist Views It." Behaviorism then became the dominant paradigm of psychology for more than 50 years, and the only subject matter deemed appropriate for study became behavior, rather than the mind.

Wilhelm Wundt (1832–1920). A German psychologist who is generally considered to be the father of experimental psychology; in 1879, he converted his demonstration laboratory into the first psychological laboratory for collecting empirical data. This laboratory served as a model for psychology and led psychology from being a discipline based in philosophy to one based in science.

Bibliography

Readings:

American Psychiatric Association. *Diagnostic and Statistical Manual of Mental Disorders*, 4th ed. Washington, DC: American Psychiatric Association, 2000. The official system used by psychiatrists and most mental health professionals and insurance companies for classifying mental illnesses.

Appley, M. H. "Motivation, equilibrium, and stress." In *Nebraska Symposium on Motivation,* 1990, edited by R. Diensthier, 1–67. Lincoln: University of Nebraska Press, 1991. A chapter discussing advances in the topic of motivation.

Beck, A. T. "Cognitive therapy." In *American Psychologist* 46 (1991): 368–375. An article by Aaron Beck, one of the founders of cognitive therapy, describing that therapy with an emphasis on cognitive restructuring.

Brottman, M. "The Two Freuds." In *The Chronicle of Higher Education*, L, no. 44 (2004): B5. An article that discusses the value of Freud's writings from mental health, literary, and philosophical perspectives.

Buss, D. M. *Evolutionary Psychology: The New Science of the Mind*, 2nd ed. Boston, MA: Pearson Education, 2004. A textbook covering most topics in evolutionary psychology.

Butcher, J. N., S. Mineka, and J. M. Hooley. *Abnormal Psychology*, 12th ed. Boston: Pearson Education, 2004. A general textbook covering various mental disorders and their treatments.

Chance, P. *Learning and Behavior*. Pacific Grove, CA: Wadsworth Publishing, 2002. A textbook covering the basic principles of learning.

Chomsky, N. *Knowledge of Language*. New York: Praeger, 1986. A book by a famous linguist making his case that the learning of language is far more sophisticated than would be predicted by the rules of operant conditioning.

Cialdini, R. B. *Influence: The Psychology of Persuasion*, rev. ed. New York: Quill, 1993. The bestselling trade book that details the social psychological research supporting the six proposed triggering mechanisms of influence.

———. "The science of persuasion." In *Scientific American* 284 (2001): 76–81. A readable article covering the basics of research on persuasion.

Cloud, J. "New sparks over electroshock." In *Time*, February 26, 2001: 60–62. An article in the popular media discussing the controversial aspects of ECT.

Coren, S., L. M. Ward, and J. T. Enns. *Sensation and Perception*, 6th ed. Fort Worth, TX: Harcourt Brace, 2004. A comprehensive textbook giving coverage to most topics in modern perception.

Creswell, J. W. *Research Design: Qualitative, Quantitative, and Mixed Methods Approaches*, 2nd ed. Thousand Oaks, CA: Sage Publications, 2003. A textbook with a comprehensive discussion of qualitative design methods.

Crews, F. C. *Unauthorized Freud.* New York: Viking, 1998. A book highly critical of Freud's theories and methods.

Daly, M., and M. Wilson. *Homicide.* Hawthorne, NY: Aldine, 1988. A classic book by two major thinkers in evolutionary psychology; examines the causes of homicide from an evolutionary perspective using several large databases from major cities.

Darwin, C. *On the Origin of Species.* London: Murray, 1859. The original book that first proposed the theory of evolution.

Dupré, J. *Human Nature and the Limits of Science.* Oxford: Clarendon Press, 2001. A book that offers arguments doubting whether the theory of evolution holds much hope in explaining human behavior.

Ellis, A. "Rational-emotive therapy." In *Current Psychotherapies*, edited by R. J. Corsini and D. Wedding, 197–238. Itasca, IL: Peacock, 1989. A chapter describing rational-emotive therapy by its founder.

Fink, M. "Electroshock revisited." In *American Scientist* 88 (2000): 162–167. An article covering the history and modern use of ECT.

Freud, S. *Introductory Lectures on Psychoanalysis.* New York: Boni and Liveright, 1924. Freud lays out all the concepts of psychoanalysis.

Gaulin, Steven J. C., and Donald H. McBurney. *Psychology: An Evolutionary Approach.* Upper Saddle River, NJ: Prentice Hall, 2001. A textbook that applies evolutionary thinking to the topics covered in most introductory psychology courses.

Gottesman, I. I. "Psychopathology through a life span-genetic prism." In *American Psychologist* 56 (2001): 867–878. An article examining the evidence that schizophrenia is a strongly genetically influenced disorder.

Hess, E. H. "The role of pupil size in communication." In *Scientific American* (November 1975): 110–119. A paper describing early research on the effect of emotion on pupil size.

Jamison, K. R. *Touched with Fire: Manic-Depressive Illness and the Artistic Temperament.* New York: Free Press Macmillan, 1993. A book detailing the interactions of bipolar disorder, creativity, and suicide.

Kalat, J. W. *Biological Psychology,* 8th ed. Pacific Grove, CA: Wadsworth-Thompson Learning, 2003. A comprehensive text covering biological psychology; included here for its coverage of the biological effects of psychoactive drugs.

————. *Introduction to Psychology,* 7th ed. Pacific Grove, CA: Wadsworth-Thompson Learning, 2005. A comprehensive introduction to most topics in psychology.

Kazdin, A. E. *Research Design in Clinical Psychology,* 4th ed. Needham Heights, MA: Allyn & Bacon, 2002. A comprehensive text on research designs, with particular emphasis on behavior therapies and token economies.

Lilienfeld, S. O., S. J. Lynn, I. Kirsch, J. F. Chaves, T. R. Sarbin, G. K. Ganaway, and R. A. Puwell. "Dissociative identity disorder and the sociocognitive model: Recalling lessons of the past." In *Psychological Bulletin* 125 (1999): 507–523. An article discussing the controversial classification of dissociative identity disorder (multiple personalities).

Loftus, E. "Our changeable memories: Legal and practical implications." In *Nature Reviews Neuroscience* 4 (2003): 231–234. An article by the leading researcher of false memories detailing the implications of her work for real-world situations.

Lovaas, O. I. *The Autistic Child: Language Development through Behavior Modification.* New York: Halsted Press, 1977. A full description of the behavior therapy program devised by Ivar Lovaas for teaching language to severely autistic children.

Martin, D. W. *Doing Psychology Experiments*, 6th ed. Pacific Grove, CA: Wadsworth-Thompson Learning, 2004. A basic guide to the steps required to conduct psychological experiments.

———. "Engineering Psychology." In *Introduction to Applied Psychology*, edited by W. L. Gregory and W. J. Burroughs, 42–74. Glenview, IL: Scott, Foresman, 1989. A chapter discussing the content and methods of engineering psychology.

Maslow, A. H. *The Farther Reaches of Human Nature*. New York: Viking Press, 1971. A book discussing in detail Maslow's theory of motivation that should lead to self-actualization.

Maudsley, H. *Body and Mind: An Inquiry into Their Connection and Mutual Influence, Specially in Reference to Mental Disorders*. London: Macmillan and Co., 1870. A historical book that mentions the unconscious mind years before Freud's introduction of the concept.

Milgram, S. *Obedience to Authority*. New York: Harper & Row, 1974. A book by the researcher who performed the famous experiments on authority involving the supposed administration of electrical shocks; describes these experiments and others.

Miller, G. A. "The magical number seven, plus or minus two: Some limits on our capacity for processing information." In *Psychological Review* 63 (1956): 81–97. One of the most widely cited journal articles in the history of psychology that summarizes research on the limits of the human ability to process information and to remember things.

Morris, D. *The Naked Ape*. New York: Dell Publishing, 1967. Written by a zoologist, this is one of the earliest books on the possibility of human behavior being at least partly explained by evolutionary principles.

Myers, D. G. "The funds, friends, and faith of happy people." In *American Psychologist* 55, no. 1 (2000): 56–67. An article that summarizes the work of Myers, Diener, and others on the variables that influence people's reported happiness worldwide.

Nathan, P. E., and J. M. Gorman, eds. *A Guide to Treatments That Work*. New York: Oxford University Press, 1998. An edited book that discusses the efficacy of therapeutic interventions.

Neath, I., and A. Surprenaut. *Human Memory*, 2nd ed. Pacific Grove, CA: Wadsworth Publishing, 2003. A comprehensive textbook that puts the modern findings about memory in historical context.

Nye, R. D. *Three Psychologies: Perspectives from Freud, Skinner, and Rogers*, 4th ed. Belmont, CA: Brooks/Cole, 1992. A book that offers a thorough treatment of Freud and his psychoanalytic theory.

Pinker, S. *The Blank Slate: The Modern Denial of Human Nature*. New York: Penguin Group, 2002. An elegantly written book attempting to explain the political and psychological reluctance of people to abandon concepts such as "the blank slate," "the noble savage," and "the ghost within."

Prochaska, J. O., and J. C. Norcross. *Systems of Psychotherapy*, 5th ed. Pacific Grove, CA: Brooks/Cole, 2003. A good review of modern psychodynamic theories since classic psychoanalysis.

Purvis, D., and R. B. Lotto. *Why We See What We Do: An Empirical Theory of Vision*. Sunderland, MA: Sinauer Associates, 2003. A book that proposes a theory based upon strong, natural, environmental cues of vision being used to build models of the world.

Santrock, J. W. *A Topical Approach to Life-Span Development*, 2nd ed. Boston: McGraw-Hill, 2005. A textbook giving comprehensive coverage to developmental psychology from a lifespan perspective.

Schachter, S., and L. Wheeler. "Epinephrine, chlorpromazine and amusement." In *Journal of Abnormal and Social Psychology* 65 (1962): 121–128. A journal article that describes some of the original work leading to the cognitive-labeling theory of emotion.

Schacter, D. L. *Searching for Memory: The Brain, the Mind, and the Past*. New York: Basic Books, 1996. A book discussing modern memory findings and theory.

Schultz, D. P., and S. E. Schultz. *A History of Modern Psychology*, 7th ed. New York: Harcourt Brace Jovanovich, 2000. A textbook on the history and systems of psychology.

Shadish, W. R., T. D. Cook, and D. T. Campbell. *Experimental and Quasi-experimental Designs for Generalized Causal Inference*. Boston: Houghton Mifflin, 2000. A guide to the use of quasi-experimental designs in which full random selection of subjects is not possible.

Skinner, B. F. "Can Psychology Be a Science of Mind?" In *American Psychologist* 45, no. 11 (1990): 1206–1210. One of the last articles written by the father of operant conditioning before he died; argues for the behaviorist tradition and against the up-and-coming trend toward cognitive psychology.

Stanovich, K. E. *How to Think Straight about Psychology*, 7th ed. Boston, MA: Pearson Education, 2004. A somewhat humorous introduction to the logic of research in psychology.

Strongman, K. T. *The Psychology of Emotion*. New York: Wiley, 1996. A textbook giving comprehensive coverage to various theories of emotion.

Sue, D., D. W. Sue, and S. Sue. *Understanding Abnormal Behavior*, 6th ed. Boston, MA: Houghton Mifflin, 2000. A basic text that covers both mental illnesses and therapies.

Todes, D. "From the machine to the ghost within: Pavlov's transition from digestive physiology to conditional reflexes." In *American Psychologist* 9 (1997): 947-955. An article by a professor in the history of medicine detailing the historical departures Pavlov made from the traditions of the contemporary researchers of his time.

Vonnegut, M. *The Eden Express*. New York: Praeger, 1975. A book that details the experiences of Mark Vonnegut (Kurt Vonnegut's son) during his bout with schizophrenia. He offers a view counter to that of his contemporaries, who argued that the mentally ill are confined and drugged for largely political reasons.

Weiner, I. B. *Principles of Psychotherapy*, 2nd ed. New York: John Wiley & Sons, 1998. A comprehensive account of what goes on during classic psychoanalysis.

Wickens, C. D., S. E. Gordon, and Y. Liu. *An Introduction to Human Factors Engineering*. New York: Addison Wesley Longman, 1997. A textbook covering the many areas of human factors engineering, including engineering psychology.

Wolpe, J. *The Practice of Behavior Therapy*, 3rd ed. Elmsford, NY: Pergamon Press, 1982. An early text by one of the founders of behavior therapy.

Internet Resources:

Cosmides, Leda, and John Tooby, Center for Evolutionary Psychology, University of California—Santa Barbara. "Evolutionary

Psychology: A Primer."
http://www.psych.ucsb.edu/research/cep/primer.html. An article by two of the founders of evolutionary psychology that gives a nice overview of the field.

Drugstory.org,
http://www.drugstory.org/drug_stats/druguse_stats.asp. This website has several sources of the most up-to-date drug-use trends.

HaidtLab: Research on Morality, Emotion, and Culture. http://www.people.virginia.edu/~haidtlab/. From this page you can link to articles by Jonathan Haidt of the University of Virginia, including one discussing the moral emotions. There are many other interesting articles on this site as well.

Human Behavior and Evolution Society. http://hbes.com. This website offers an introduction to the field of evolutionary psychology, including videos and a book chapter, and allows one to participate in Web-based research.

Human Factors and Ergonomics Society. http://www.hfes.org/. This website provides information about the field and the society and has recent articles in the news highlighting research in this area.

Loftus, Elizabeth. "Creating False Memories." http://faculty.washington.edu/ eloftus/Articles/sciam.htm. An article written for *Scientific American*.

Lorayne, Harry. "Memory Training and Memory Improvement." http://www.harrylorayne.com/. A website that advertises and has demonstrations of some of the techniques taught by Harry Lorayne, one of the best-known teachers of mnemonic devices.

"A Primer of Imaging in Psychiatry." http://www.musc.edu/psychiatry/ fnrd/primer_index.htm. This is a website meant for psychiatrists that contains several tutorial articles explaining the basics of brain-scanning techniques.

Purves-Lab, Laboratory of Dale Purves, M.D., Center for Cognitive Neuroscience, Duke University. www.purveslab.net. Dale Purves's website demonstrates many visual illusions.

Timmons, Robin, and Leonard Hamilton. "Drugs, brains and behavior." www.rci.rutgers.edu/~lwh/drugs/. A website containing a complete basic text on drugs from 1990; provided by the authors for free use.

Visual Cognition Laboratory, University of Illinois. Viscog.beckman.uiuc.edu/ djs_lab/demos.html. A website demonstrating visual and attentional illusions.

Williams, David. "The Desmond Morris Information Page." http://www.desmond-morris.com/. A website containing a biography of Desmond Morris, author of *The Naked Ape*, along with a listing of books, research articles, and even artwork.